The Gloucester & Sharpness Canal

and

Robert Mylne

Christopher Gotch

The signature in the title is reproduced from a letter by
Robert Mylne.

First Edition 1993

© Christopher Gotch

ISBN 0-9518011-1-2

Printed by The Lantern Press
45, Nero Court, Brentford Dock,
Brentford, Middlesex. TW8 8QB

Gloucester. 1793.

CONTENTS

Frontispiece

Notes at the end of each chapter

PREFACE

This history of the construction of the Gloucester and Sharpness Canal, as opposed to the history of Gloucester Docks, induced me to use it as a means to restore the reputation of Robert Mylne, a prodigy of his era. It has long been a cause dear to me to rectify the unfair neglect afforded Mylne.

In doing so, however, some may consider I have been less than just to Charles Hadfield, the venerable canal historian whose scholarship in many books has been echoed by that of other authors commissioned by him in his role as publisher and editor.

Without their researches I could not have provided the evidence to resuscitate Mylne's long-tarnished reputation, and it is no less than irony that Hadfield and Skempton should have been the main source. There is a further irony.

Some twenty years back I submitted to David and Charles (Hadfield's firm of Publishers) a manuscript called 'Herons Lifting', a diverse mixture of canal history and personal experience of canal cruising, somewhat difficult to categorise. It was rejected; yet it contained much of the material on Robert Mylne utilised in this book.

Consequently no accusation can be made justifiably that I have been harsh on Hadfield. Harsh on Jessop, yes, for only in so doing could Mylne be rehabilitated and, after all, the whole matter of 'Nailing the Lie' is now academic. The issue is simply one of bias between biographers for their own subjects.

I have hinted strongly that Hadfield's championship of Jessop resulted in malignity towards Mylne but in proving my case the reverse seems apparent too. But in any trial there must be a loser and for two centuries Mylne has been convicted as a perjurer.

Now, on appeal, the verdict has been overturned and Mylne's evidence has been upheld. My only issue with Hadfield and his bevy of commissioned canal historians, if commissioned they were, is that the evidence existed in fact but never processed.

On Mylne's behalf points of importance are in bold text, the emphasis being mine.

For example, Upton's "Observations on the Gloucester and Sharpness Canal. 1815." has long been available but for some reason dismissed; presumably because Upton himself was later dismissed. Yet his evidence remains valid: it is simply a matter of interpretation.

This book is more than just the history of a canal timed as part of British Waterways' Canals 200 celebration in 1993. It fulfils in some degree a wish expressed by Tony Conder, Curator of the National Waterways Museum.

> "The closer people come to the truth of engineers' characters the happier I shall be. Most canal 'names' are very two-dimensional. We know they exist and we have an idea of what they built. It is very rare to get a glimpse of the personality behind the facts."

If, by achieving this at the expense of a bruised toe or two, canal history can reach a wider readership, so much the better.

Christopher Gotch
1993

INTRODUCTION

The Canal Mania of the late 18th century peaked in 1793. That year thirty-two canal acts were passed - a record number. The Gloucester and Berkeley (Sharpness) Canal Act was one. The shortest at under twenty miles, it surpassed all others in width and depth to allow passage of vessels of "300 tons burthen", between the Severn at Berkeley Pill and the "Port of Gloucester". Hence its importance. Most canals had a chequered history of construction, but this one more than most. It took 34 years to complete and a further 44 years before free from mortgage. Subsequently adapted for 1000 ton ships, commercial use has now dwindled. Even the Manchester Ship Canal, for which it was the model, constructed nearly a century later has been abandoned as a commercial waterway.

The merchants of Gloucester had long realised the potential of the river Severn as a trade route and of their city as an inland port for trans-shipment between the Midland industrial areas and Bristol. Resenting, however, the commercial dominance of Bristol as a seaport, they sought means to obviate this. The new form of canal transport provided an answer, almost by chance, when Benjamin Grazebrook, a merchant of nearby Stroud, formed a short canal to join the Severn at Framilode in 1779. This inspired them with the idea of a direct route to London rather than Bristol.

It also inspired them around 1783 to contemplate bypassing the Severn's tortuous bends and treacherous sandbanks, with a canal large enough for sea-going vessels. A bold conception this; so bold it took a decade to germinate. No-one knows who conceived it first, or planned the line; it may have been contrived in committee. But in 1791 or thereabout, Josiah Clowes, the resident engineer of the Thames and Severn Canal produced the first technical drawing of the line, since vanished.

The Act for the Canal was passed in 1793 under the aegis of Robert Mylne, the foremost civil engineer - and architect - of that period, an expert in such matters. With all set fair for an early completion of this grandiose venture, what then went wrong? A strange story this, one clamouring to be told. Not so much a history as a "Whodunnit" mystery with character assassination and Robert Mylne, the canal's one and only Chief Engineer, as victim. His reputation, postmortem, has never recovered and is still impugned today by canal historians.

This story is one of incompetence, greed, arrogance, conflict, conspiracy and corruption clutching within its maw proprietors, engineers and contractors alike. Whatever his faults Robert Mylne can be exonerated, for the finger of suspicion which he, himself, first raised (to be mocked subsequently by historians) must be levelled now at the "hero" of the Canal boom; none other than William Jessop.

"How can this be?" pundits may well ask, "Jessop had little to do with the Gloucester and Sharpness Canal." Indirectly a great deal as will be related. He not only knew Mylne - and Mylne knew him all too well - but Telford too and Telford was, ex-offico, the other Chief Engineer of the canal who brought it to fruition; after the conspiracies had ceased and those involved were dead.

The story of this canal cannot be told in isolation for the world of Canal Mania involved a surprisingly small group of adventurers, specialists of indeterminate quality and artisans often led by unscrupulous charlatans. The wonder of it all, especially in this year of British Waterways 200 celebrations, is that so many canals reached completion, in the face of incredible odds. Two hundred years ago the Gloucester and Sharpness Canal became a possibility.

This is the story of how it became a reality.

1

GERMINATION

Between the idea
And the reality
Between the motion
And the act
Falls the Shadow.
                    (Thomas Stearns Eliot)

The events that overtook the Gloucester and Sharpness Canal in the first few years are reflected in much of the history of what has been termed the Thames and Severn Canal. This in fact was the amalgamation of two navigations, the Stroudwater and the Thames and Severn, opened finally in 1792 for through traffic even though bedevilled by the inadequacy of the Thames navigation to London.

Many of those involved reappear in the story of the Gloucester and Sharpness Canal, and the faults and problems with which they had to contend were repeated, as if experience counted for nought.

There was one difference, however, in that the finance for the Thames and Severn came mainly from London shareholders, even though the project was controlled by local men such as Benjamin Grazebrook, sometime brewer, navigation carrier and self-professed surveyor and engineer who brought water supplies to Stroud. In 1774 he was one of nine "undertakers" for a canal to bypass the river Frome and its many mills and thus bring trade from the river Severn to Stroud. These promoters sought advice from Thomas Yeoman[1], a London Engineer of repute, who checked the line and approved the scheme.

Work began in 1775 at Framilode on the lock from the river Severn. Four years later the seven miles and thirteen locks to Stroud had been completed and by 1785 the cut as far as Chalford also opened.

Meanwhile the Thames and Severn Canal Company had been formed after a meeting in Cirencester in 1781 with Edward Loveden[2] in the chair. The exact line to and junction with the Thames caused controversy, between that to Lechlade via Cirencester against one to Cricklade. The former with a branch cut to Cirencester won the day.

As Yeoman had died meanwhile, Robert Whitworth's[3] opinion was sought. The Company recorded later that "Robert Whitworth was not at any time the acting Surveyor and Engineer", so the design of the Thames and Severn Canal cannot be attributed to him, as other canal historians have long maintained.

Like Yeoman previously, Whitworth checked the surveys already carried out, but had such reservations that he re-surveyed the summit level. Due to pressure of work, he took a year to submit his report for which he charged a mere eighteen guineas.

The enabling act, passed in 1783, was based on a plan of the line marked out by Grazebrook. It seems that Whitworth, although repeatedly requested, never did confirm the line except for Sapperton Tunnel. Undeterred, the Canal Committee sanctioned work to commence.

James Perry, a Wolverhampton merchant, shareholder and committee member, decided upon an extended sabbatical to take charge of the works. Before long the committee, realising his value, awarded him a salary as ex-offico Superintendent. Perry lost no time in appointing a supervisory team and controlling rates for the work force. He became, in effect, the Clerk to the Canal Company. As such, he engaged Josiah Clowes[4] as Surveyor, [resident] Engineer and Head Carpenter at £300 p.a. whose duties included assisting "Mr Whitworth the surveyor in setting out the Navigation" as duly minuted and thus causing confusion to historians.

To record contracts, check materials and quantities, pay wages and bills, Perry appointed Samuel Smith of Stourbridge as Clerk of Works at £120 p.a. So efficient was Smith that, had he been employed on the Gloucester and Sharpness Canal later, many troubles might have been avoided. Richard Hall[5], "a local surveyor of repute", accepted the post of assistant Clerk of the Works "whose duties were to check the level before and after excavation and measure the work of the canal cutters"[6].

Promoted "at the desire of several opulent private persons, chiefly merchants of London ... who had no local interest"[7], the Thames and Severn Canal appeared to be in sound hands. James Perry himself invested a small fortune, hardly matching one subscription of £23,000 and several others of £10,000 apiece, so intended to assure it bore fruit. Out-classed by such metropolitan wealth, most proprietors of the Stroudwater Canal opted out.

To prevent delays - crucial to avoid wasteful expenditure - Perry purchased land for the line in advance with immediate cash settlements. Failing this, the process necessitated arbitration by independent land valuers; worse still, reference to the Commissioners (County residents) named in the Act. Delays could be incalculable and detrimental always to progress: another lesson the the Gloucester and Sharpness Committee should have learned later.

For cutting the canal, a piecework system operated by agreement with gang leaders, two of whom were Thomas Cook and John Pickston or Pinxston, notorious for scamped work especially clay puddling.

Under such efficient management the Thames and Severn Canal, notwithstanding the difficult Sapperton tunnel 3,817 yards long (exceeded only by two other canal tunnels), was completed in under ten years, a record achievement at the time and highly satisfactory to all investors.

Yet problems emerged. In operation the canal suffered acute water shortage and the river Thames, to which it was now linked and dependent upon for trade with London, proved inadequate for easy navigation.

Grazebrook,[8] not Whitworth, designed the Thames and Severn Canal and, with Perry and Clowes, altered the line as work proceeded not always to advantage. Such were the problems after opening two leading engineers, Smeaton[9] and Mylne, were asked to report upon deficiencies.

Both reported adversely on lack of water feeders to the summit and criticised the rise and spacing of locks, a cause of water wastage. Smeaton's report was almost the last he made before he died in November 1792.

Lord Eliot, a local landowner whose water the Company had filched, actually commissioned Smeaton. He forwarded to Perry a copy of the Report, with a scathing comment on "the want of knowledge in the very first principals [sic] of canal making" by the proprietors.

The latter in defence turned to Mylne in September 1793, shortly before he was appointed Chief Engineer to the proposed Gloucester and Sharpness Canal, for his report assuming it would prove favourable.

As Household[10] states fallaciously; "It was unkind of Robert Mylne (in a pique after surveying another line of canal to Cirencester and subsequently learning that Whitworth had advised against any further canal cutting through the Cotswolds) to imply, as he did, that the 'erroneous system and subsequent fatal Deficiencies' of the Thames and Severn Canal arose from Proprietors and busy men becoming engineers, self-made, and handling subjects of the most dangerous kind!"

Household missed the point. Mylne was attacking not Whitworth, not Perry, but Grazebrook. The latter surveyed, marked the line and decided upon locks and pound spacing. Grazebrook, too, proposed the canal from Bristol, not to Cirencester as such, but to join the Gloucester and Sharpness near Halmer Green and thence, via the Thames and Severn, to Cirencester (as originally intended). He met Mylne to discuss this in September 1793 and again in 1794, when Mylne represented the Gloucester and Sharpness Company. After lengthy negotiations with Grazebrook, Mylne rejected the plan unless certain conditions were met.

His report on the Thames and Severn Canal was as outspoken as it was correct. Due to water shortage the canal was doomed, even after the problem of the Thames had been solved, by none other than Mylne.

William Jessop[11] now enters the fray; Edward Loveden, shareholder in both the Thames and Severn and the Gloucester and Sharpness, was the activist. All traffic was obliged to pass through the twenty-five miles of the Upper Thames, including Buscot Lock owned by

Loveden who levied a monstrous toll. As early as 1789, the Thames and Severn Company tackled the problem of the Upper Thames Navigation and forced Loveden, and his fellow commissioners for that stretch of the river, to take action. They called in "William Jessop who recommended, inter alia, the erection of eight pound locks and no less than fifty-five timber bridges for the towing path."[12]

This was in 1791 but within a matter of months, four locks collapsed. Later that year Loveden called upon Mylne who, from then until 1802, transformed the Thames, as described by Thacker in his two volumes on the Thames. No mention is made by Hadfield and Skempton[13] of the failure of Jessop's locks. They present a different version.

> "On 1st April 1791, the first stage of the improvements completed, the Commissioners, clearly pleased with Jessop's earlier work, wanted him to look over what had been done and suggest further improvements. But he was too busy, and Mylne did it instead."

The Thames, being one of the contributory causes of the conception of the Thames and Severn Canal, and even more so of the Grand Junction canal, it is necessary to examine this important waterway especially as Mylne was instrumental in procuring the many improvements that render it still a vital link in water navigation today. One would have liked to have said waterborne commercial traffic but that has now ceased.

Mylne's association with the river dates from before 1790 and it seems probable that, like the Gloucester and Sharpness, he owed his appointment to Edward Loveden. The latter, as owner of a large estate on the Thames at Buscot, was one of the many commissioners of the Thames navigation, the Upper Thames in this instance. And so it was that Mylne in his capacity of Engineering Consultant "went up the Thames in the Navigation barge to Staines to view the works to improvement in August 1790". In April the following year, making Buscot his base, he carried out an extensive survey of the upper reaches of the river from Inglesham, where the Thames and Severn Canal joined it, down to Abingdon, extending this to include the lower reaches as far as Reading. Once again, Hadfield tilts at Mylne.

> "Early in 1791 the commissioners told the private weir owners between Lechlade and Oxford to put them in proper repair and then, having authorised more expenditure on the upper river, called in Jessop to re-survey in the light of what had already been done. He was too busy, and the cantankerous elderly Robert Mylne did the work, his temper not improved by being asked because Jessop, whom he disliked, had been too busy. Mylne recommended the replacement of 25 weirs and flash-locks between Lechlade and Abingdon by a smaller number of pound locks, the purchase of the old locks, a continuous towing path and a deeper channel. He was downright in his opinions …."

It was the private ownership of the Thames weirs that bedevilled the navigation for the commissioners had no control over them. Since many of the weir owners were also mill owners who needed water for milling, there was obviously a dichotomy here in the right of water - the millers or the boatmen. Whereas Hadfield maintains, incorrectly, that Mylne first acted for the commissioners in 1791 as a substitute for Jessop (Mylne's first diary entry is for 1790), Thacker[14] records that

> "about this time (1788) when Thames navigation appeared at length in a fair way to pass under efficient public control, Robert Mylne emerges as surveyor to the commission; a man of many ideas, not all acceptable……. it was due to his persistent recommendations that in 1791 they began, under their statutory powers, to purchase the private weirs. A beginning was to be made with those adjoining the new pound locks." [Thacker also makes a pertinent point regarding Mylne as a character.] "I would again remark in passing upon the humanity of this Robert Mylne, which appears more than once in the excuses he embodies in his reports for the free-holders of some of these weirs, who through poverty could not afford to rebuild them."

During the summer of 1793, Mylne found himself a principal figure in an indictment of the Thames Commissioners. An enquiry was held at which he gave evidence both on the state of the river and upon the actions of its guardians, evidence of an uncomplimentary nature, for he noted that these items i.e. his services, "could not be paid for by the

Commissioners of the Thames as it was to show the impropriety of their conduct."[15] The enquiry was conducted by a committee of the House of Commons which, after evidence from both sides, expressed the view that "by reference to the Journals of the House, it would appear that the Commissioners of the Five Upper districts have opposed every Attempt at Improvement by Canal; the Evidence given to your committee affords abundant testimony of their Negligence in endeavouring to perfect the River."

The Thames and Severn was well subscribed yet Whitworth, in his brief association with it, submitted an estimate for completion not far short of the total sum listed in the enabling Act. This shocked the shareholders for, even before the canal opened in record time, the share capital was exhausted "but also the £60,000 authorised to borrow on mortgage, and power to borrow another £60,000 on similar terms to complete ... the canal, ... obtained in 1791."[16] Furthermore it proved impossible to pay interest in full out of capital. "Very few proprietors troubled to keep a watch on the company's affairs." They left matters to the committee, as did the Gloucester and Sharpness Canal soon after with dire results. By 1802-3, these matters came to a head resulting in the election of a permanent chairman, John Disney junior,[17] a barrister holding many shares and a considerable mortgage.

It took several years to evolve a solution but, by 1809, the situation had improved, yet the canal never proved successful financially. Its death throes were prolonged for it was not finally abandoned until 1933. Household sums up the ludicrous situation whereby "Every Canal Company hoped that the share capital would suffice to equip (i.e. construct) the line and, in addition, provide a dividend of 5% p.a. UNTIL revenue should be earned." He maintains this to have been common practice and "encouraged proprietors to subscribe promptly ... and provide an incentive to complete the works ... quickly and economically".

The Gloucester and Sharpness Canal Company, such was the greed of proprietors[18], doubled dividends to 10% p.a. and when, inevitably, money ran out turned upon their Chief Engineer and dismissed him. That man was Robert Mylne.[19]

NOTES

1   THOMAS YEOMAN (1708-1781)
    Joint engineer with Smeaton 1754 for River Lea Navigation. Involved with the Coventry Canal and consultant for the Stroudwater Canal and Forth and Clyde navigation. First President of The Smeatonian Society (1771-1781) with Mylne as Vice-President.

2   EDWARD LOVEDEN
    Upper Thames Commissioner who held the toll rights - as owner of Buscot Park - of St. John's lock, Lechlade. Shareholder of Thames and Severn and Gloucester and Sharpness Canal Companies. Jessop, as engineer to improve the Upper Thames, 1786-1791, knew him well until four of six new locks collapsed. Loveden then turned to Mylne who carried out permanent improvements 1791-1806, still valid today.

3   ROBERT WHITWORTH (1734-1799)
    James Brindley's principal assistant - and son-in-law - from 1767 until Brindley's death in 1771. Spent most of his life completing Brindley's canals but in demand as a Consultant on many other navigations in competition with Jessop and in association. He also worked with Mylne on the proposed London Canal (never constructed). Joined The Smeatonian Society at the second meeting. Surveyed the Lower Thames in 1771 and the Thames and Severn Canal 1783 and 1784. In 1795 he took over the Hereford and Gloucester Canal from Clowes.

4   JOSIAH (Josias; Joseph) CLOWES (1735-1795)
    Engineer of the Thames and Severn 1783-1789, the Hereford and Gloucester 1790 and the Shrewsbury Canal 1793, he is listed by Hadfield as obtaining enabling Acts in 1791 and two in 1793. It is possible he surveyed the line of the Bristol and Cirencester Canal for Benjamin Grazebrook in 1792 and the first line of the Gloucester and Sharpness in 1790. His salary as engineer of the Thames and Severn in 1793, was £300 p.a. compared with Mylne's salary of £350 p.a. in 1793 as Chief Engineer of the Gloucester and Sharpness. Never a member of The Smeatonian Society.

5   RICHARD HALL
     Land Surveyor of Gloucester in partnership with Thomas Pinnell who signed the earliest extant drawings of the Gloucester and Sharpness Canal in 1792.

6   Thames and Severn Canal. H. Household. 1969. David and Charles.

7   Phillips. General History of Inland Navigation. 1803.

8   BENJAMIN GRAZEBROOK
     Instigator of the Stroudwater Canal, and of the Thames and Severn too. Certainly proposed the Bristol and Cirencester Canal (unbuilt), the line of which passed through Lord Berkeley's land. Assumed to be a shareholder of the Gloucester and Sharpness Canal Company, it was vital to him and his associates for the line to terminate at Berkeley Pill. No doubt sought advice from Daniel Lysons junior, the topographer, and thus established the anti-Mylne clique. This is conjecture.

9   JOHN SMEATON (1724-1792)
     See DNB. for career. Studied engineering in Holland 1754, where Mylne followed in 1758-9. He and Mylne worked together, especially on the Tyne Bridges, when Jessop was still his pupil. Acknowledged leader of Civil Engineers in the widest sense, not just canals, and succeeded as such by Mylne after his death. With Mylne founded the Smeatonian Society.

10   Ibid. 6.

11   William Jessop (1745-1814)
     Devon born, trained by Smeaton who then pased on excess commissions. Only after the latter's death in 1792 was Jessop accepted as a leading canal engineer in his own right. As such his career proved short for, after 1806, ill-health confined his work to arbitration. Chief Engineer of the Ellesmere, Caledonian and Grand Junction Canals.

12   Ibid. 6.

13   William Jessop. Hadfield and Skempton. 1979. David and Charles.

14   History of The River Thames. Thacker.

15   Mylne's Journals. 1762-1810.
     Mylne's Business Journals from 1762 to 1810 have survived. They were in diary format, one week on the left hand page with an account sheet to the right. He noted receipts and disbursements meticulously on the account sheet but also noted expenses and fees to be charged against relevant daily entries but omitted pound signs if the figure quoted was in guineas. The excerpts quoted have been confined to the subject of this book with a few pertinent additions. The spelling of names is erratic, and the term 'dining' referred to the mid-day meal. Account entries are in brackets.

16   Ibid. 6.

17   JOHN DISNEY Junior
     Local wealthy man of influence and shareholder in both Thames and Severn and Gloucester and Sharpness Canal Companies who favoured Mylne.

18   Mylne bought ten £100 shares in the Canal Company. This represented over double his annual fees as Chief Engineer - a not inconsiderable sum then thus confirming his belief in the venture at the start, but not for long. However the 10% dividend on this relatively modest investment, in August 1796 amounting to £140 (See Appendix ii), must have shocked him and confirmed his contention, made clear to the Proprietors, that such payment, prior to any income received, was tantamount to madness.

19   Ibid. 15.

2

THE CHIEF ENGINEER

"A rare jintleman - hot as pepper and proud as Lucifer"
(A Navigation Cutter)

The Thames and Severn Canal enabling Act of 1783 galvanised the merchants and bankers of Gloucester into action. Deliberation is more accurate. They formed a canal committee that year. This proposed a basin - more a haven really - (immediately to the north of the existing Dock) simply as a trans-shipment point between Worcester, Bristol and the entrance to the Stroudwater Canal at Framilode.

This attempt to emphasise Gloucester's claim as a port failed because the land for the basin had been earmarked for the new county gaol. A mere connection with the Stroudwater, limiting size of craft, was dismissed in favour of a radical proposal for, not a boat but a ship canal, "seventeen and three quarter miles long to circumvent the 35 mile navigational hazard on the River Severn between the same points to induce traffic from the Severn to the canal", never before envisaged nor attempted. No wonder deliberations were prolonged.

Not all the invited shareholders were local - the project was too large for that - and those of London and elsewhere demanded a national figure amongst civil engineers to obtain the enabling Act. Smeaton, the most renowned engineer in his time, had died so the next obvious choice could be none other than Robert Mylne,[1] his successor as leader of the profession and, at that time, leader of the architectural profession too, for Robert Adam also had died in 1792.

No one man before had been acclaimed leader of two professions simultaneously. Only one other, Thomas Telford (1757-1834) of the next generation, was to aspire to this but never achieved equal renown in both. After Telford the two professions separated entirely. Robert Mylne therefore remains unique. However, the Gloucester and Sharpness Canal proved his Achilles heel through which his reputation - as an engineer - has been besmirched. Who then was this paragon?

Descended from a long line of Master Masons to the Crown of Scotland, Robert Mylne (1733-1811) was born in Edinburgh, and apprenticed to a carpenter and joiner; he studied architecture in Italy and engineering in Holland. He won acclaim in Rome, as the first Briton to be awarded the Silver Medal for architecture at St. Luke's Academy, and early fame in London on his return by winning the competition for the design of the third bridge over the Thames, at Blackfriars, against strong opposition from established professionals such as Sir William Chambers and John Smeaton. From then on, he never looked back; commissions for work, architectural and engineering, poured in. At first bridges predominated, but in 1767, Mylne was appointed Engineer and Surveyor to the New River Company, responsible for London's water supply brought from Hertford to Sadlers Wells, a post he held until shortly before his death when he handed over to his son, William Chadwell Mylne. In 1767 too, he was elected a Fellow of the Royal Society.

At the same time he was appointed Surveyor to no less than four Cathedrals, St Paul's London, Canterbury, Rochester and Durham.

Hitherto ignored has been Mylne's role as Canal Consultant whereby he acted, in one capacity or another, in connection with no less than a quarter of all canals planned during the canal boom. No other engineer can boast such a record, except William Jessop.

Because of his role as consultant, Mylne's contribution to canal history has been overlooked. His advice was sought either in the early stage of a project so that he might obtain, or oppose, depending upon which side he represented, the necessary Act of Parliament required, or when hazards were met during construction, or a crisis such as acute water shortage after completion. This happened with the Thames and Severn Canal by which time the remedy proposed was too late, too costly or both. Canal proprietors, when in trouble, always sought the most expert advice possible and so turned to Smeaton or Mylne for help.

Historians, quite naturally, have been concerned more with what was achieved and constructed rather than what was proposed or opposed. Thus Mylne's reputation has suffered as a result. Just as in architecture he has been overshadowed by Adam, so Rennie and Telford received credit for finishing work initiated by Mylne. Canal specialists, such as Jessop and Whitworth, figure more prominently in contemporary canal records.

Mylne's great contribution to the improvement of the Fens, the Eau Brink Cut, was completed after his death by Rennie: the Gloucester and Sharpness Canal by Telford.

A catalogue of Mylne's involvement with canals and rivers makes impressive reading. (See Appendix iii.) Apart from minor improvements to the Trent and major ones to the Severn, it was due to Mylne's persistent advocacy over nearly fifteen years, from 1790 onwards, that the Upper Thames Commissioners, notoriously lax in their guardianship of the river, were forced to improve the navigation. For once Mylne has received recognition from the Thames historian, Thacker, who devoted much of his second volume to an assessment of Mylne's reports and the improvements that followed.

Mylne's other engineering work was as wide in scope as commissions were numerous, ranging from bridges to docks, dams, harbours, piers, lighthouses, to mills and waterworks, besides surveys and reports on fisheries, fortifications, wharves, and embankments. He was in great demand too as an arbitrator in engineering disputes thus confirming his leading role in the profession. In his dual capacity of architect and engineer, he was essentially a man of both stone and water, a maker of both static and liquid history.

That he was a man of some conceit, some arrogance cannot be denied. According to his obituary he possessed "a high independence of spirit and an inflexible sense of duty" both attributes unlikely to make him popular. According to the artist, Farington, a contemporary gossip writer, Mylne "was a man much disposed to conversation and drank wine at and after his meals freely - he was extremely exact in all his affairs and lotted all his concerns with great care." Hence the invaluable Business Journals,[2] kept throughout his working life, provide evidence of his movements, clients, accounts and achievements.

Mylne has never been recognised as an innovator, yet the elliptical arches he chose for increased strength to Blackfriars bridge in 1760 created a furore at the time. He was pilloried in contemporary broadsheets by, amongst many, none other than Dr. Samuel Johnson. The innovation soon became a fashion for bridge designs to follow.

Then in 1774, when engaged upon considerable work for the 5th Duke of Argyll at Inverary, he produced an astonishing surprise. "There is one bridge design by Robert Mylne" states Ruddock[3] "which ... is probably the earliest surviving design of an iron bridge." Referred to by Mylne in his journal as "Castle or metal bridge. Cost £2,500" and never built, it predated T.F. Pritchard's iron bridge over the Severn in 1779.

An earlier bridge at Inverary, attributed to John or James Adam, is almost certainly by Mylne. Known as the garden or Frew's Bridge it is a curious hybrid. The abutment approach is totally different in style and probably designed by John Adam, elder brother of James and Robert, who preceded Mylne at Inverary working for the 4th Duke of Argyll. Now, John had designed a bridge for the Earl of Dumfries at Dumfries house in February 1760 just when Mylne's ellipses for Blackfriars Bridge caused such consternation. His brother, Robert, had known Mylne both at school in Edinburgh and in Rome. They were rivals.

It is my contention that Robert immediately prevailed upon John to use ellipses for the Dumfries Bridge, described by Ruddock as pretentious. The whole design is clumsy with an awkward rise, like the garden bridge at Inverary built 1760-61. So it is possible that John "who signed the final design" of the garden bridge had adapted this, at Robert's bidding, into an ellipse.

Yet this bridge, apart from the steep approaches, reveals an elegance uncharacteristic of John Adam. To my mind it is more likely that the Marquis of Lorne (5th Duke of Argyll 1770), then prominent in the London 'bon ton' persuaded his father to adapt the latest fashion for bridge designs for the garden bridge and sent a sketch by Mylne for this purpose.

The Castle interior decorations, long attributed to Robert Adam, are now known to have been by Mylne.[4] Indeed what has been known as the Adam style may have been introduced by Mylne himself.[5] Certainly the predominant neo-classical style of architecture in Britain in the last half of the 18th century owed as much to Mylne as to Adam, or Bonomi, Carr,

Dance the younger, Holland, Stuart or Wyatt, to whom much of his work has been attributed. No doubt Telford could be included too, for his early career as an architect reveals Mylne's influence. Sir John Soane declared, to Mylne's son, his admiration "for the taste and genius of his father".

Thus we find L.C.T. Rolt[6] suggesting, without evidence, that Telford, rather than Mylne, designed "the elegant little bridgeman's [sic] cottages on the Gloucester and Berkeley Canal, which with their classical porticoes, recall the Regency as vividly as the stucco terraces of nearby Cheltenham. These canal cottages ... are merely 'workers homes' yet they are also a last flowering of English architectural genius". To this can be added Mylne's contention, in 1760, that "When the magnificent is procured by the simple and the genuine, it pleases universally".[7]

* * * * *

The canal age owed genesis to James Brindley (1716-1772), a self-professed engineer, before that epithet was recognised. Josiah Wedgwood wrote of him in 1767 with prescience: "I am afraid he will do too much and leave us before his vast designs are executed." The Industrial Revolution generated more than just canal engineers for there were other aspects of construction, civic and commercial. Whereas Brindley concentrated upon canals his successor, John Smeaton (1724-1792), specialised in docks, harbours, bridges and lighthouses as well as canals.

His successor, in turn, Robert Mylne embraced an even wider field which included architecture. Meanwhile the pupils of both Brindley and Smeaton concentrated upon canal work; Robert Whitworth (1734-1799), Brindley's son-in-law, and William Jessop (1745-1814), Smeaton's pupil. Even older than Brindley but less well known, Thomas Yeoman constructed the world's first water-powered cotton mill in Northampton in 1743, designed roads and agricultural machinery, before turning to canal works as a consultant for the Coventry Canal, and the Stroudwater Canal projects.

In 1750, few recognised engineers existed yet two decades later seven of this new breed decided to form a dining club named The Smeatonian Society. On 15th March 1771 Yeoman was elected President. At the next meeting, a fortnight later, Mylne was elected Vice-President. Other new members were Robert Whitworth and John Golborne; both were to work closely with Mylne during the years to come.

Further names connected with the Gloucester and Sharpness venture are listed as elected members thereafter; William Jessop in 1773, William Faden (1749-1836), geographer, in 1776, John Pinkerton (Jessop's partner until 1813) of the firm of Pinkerton and Co, ubiquitous canal cutters and contractors, Thomas Dadford, (uncle or father of James Dadford the resident engineer of the Gloucester and Sharpness, 1794-1799) in 1783, and John Troughton (1739-1807), Instrument maker, in 1793.

Robert Mylne remained vice-president for seven years. In 1793, after Smeaton's death, he became treasurer - all other offices abolished - until his death in 1811. Thus, in effect, he ran the society single-handed for nigh on eighteen years. Even though a founder member of the Architects' Club in 1791, later to be The Royal Institute of British Architects (1834), for Mylne The Smeatonian Society, as it was called, proved dear to his heart. Less so perhaps some of its members.

Mylne, not Smeaton nor Yeoman, established the precepts of the Society; "Conversation, argument and a social communication of ideas and knowledge in the particular walks of each member are, at the same time, the amusement and business of the meetings in a friendly way, to shake hands together and be **personally known** to each other." Three levels of membership emerged as time went by; Civil Engineers themselves (or those who professed to be and were known as such) as the first, Honorary members as the second and "others", described by Mylne as "workmen and artificers connected with and employed in works of engineering", as the third class.[8] Faden and Troughton[9] were listed amongst the latter, even though Faden had been elected FRS, as had Mylne, Smeaton and many another but not Jessop, Whitworth nor Pinkerton.

Mylne, conscious of his role as Consultant Engineer busy with proposing or opposing

Acts of Parliament for numerous projects, especially those for canals, considered The Smeatonian Society to be of value in that: "They [the members] often met accidentally in the Houses of Parliament and in the Courts of Justice, each maintaining the propriety of his own designs without knowing much of each other. Thus the sharp edges of their minds might be rubbed off, as it were, by a closer communication of ideas, **no ways naturally hostile**."[10] The events that follow tested this statement to the utmost and found it wanting.

One blunt statement by Mylne, in a letter of 1802, sealed his fate and subsequent reputation with canal historians. He dared to call William Jessop "A common canal cutter." He went further, as will be told, to impugn Jessop's honesty and thus has been dismissed ever since as a "cantankerous" old man oozing bile and jealousy.

His success in both professions,[11] his standing with clients and professional colleagues, deny this. In addition he had, what appears to have been, a happy family life in spite of the tragic deaths of wife, several children and other close relations. His second son became a partner and twice President of The Smeatonian Society. True, his unsuccessful brother smarted from Mylne's generous - perhaps tactless - help in time of dire trouble and desperate need. And true, he was lonely in old age.

Yet his descendants, unlike Jessop's, kept intact his papers, letters and journals. They had nothing to hide. For all his human frailties Mylne was an admirable man. A contemporary maintained, at his death, that Mylne "had peculiarities in his character, but they were chiefly connected with a high independence of spirit and an inflexible sense of duty and justice. He loved his profession but not the emoluments of it and, thereafter, after all his distinguished employments did not die rich. Those who knew him could not fail to respect his integrity and admire his talents". James Elmes summed him up best by quoting the remark of a navvy (navigation cutter): "A rare jintleman, hot as pepper and proud as Lucifer."

This then was the man chosen to be Chief Engineer of the Gloucester and Sharpness Canal.

NOTES

1   Based on unpublished Thesis by Christopher Gotch and his articles published in Country Life and Architectural Review. 1953, and subsequently in Waterways World. 1979. See also Dictionary of Architects. 1640-1840. H.M. Colvin, and Shropshire. N. Pevsner.

2   Mylne's Journals. 1762-1810 (Now in RIBA Library)

3   Arch Bridges and their Builders. 1738-1835. Ted Ruddock. Cambridge University Press. 1979

4   Determined from drawings, mentioned in Mylne's Journal, by Christopher Gotch.

5   Architectural Review. C. Gotch. The Missing Years of Robert Mylne. 1951; Mylne and Inverary. 1953; Adam and Mylne 1956.

6   Inland Waterways of England. 1950. L.T.C. Rolt

7   Mylne's pamphlet on Blackfriars Bridge.

8   The Smeatonians. Garth Watson. 1989. Telford Press.

9   Faden prepared engraved maps, and Troughton, models for Mylne of the Gloucester and Sharpness Canal.

10   Ibid. 8.

11   See Appendices iii - v

3

GREAT EXPECTATIONS

"Pray for one who stands on the pinnacle of slippery fortune and the
world's esteem."

(Mylne to his Father, 1760.)

In 1795, John Phillips published his "History of Inland Navigation". Of the Gloucester and Berkeley Canal, then under construction, he wrote 'This undertaking for its magnitude and accommodations, deserves to be considered as one of the finest importance - by uniting the city of Gloucester, by an easy and certain water carriage with the port of Bristol, and from thence with all the world; it may justly be deemed an object of great magnitude to trade."

Phillips then referred to "an ardour of enterprise" on the part of those who had conceived the undertaking and set it in motion - the merchants and bankers of Gloucester. Regrettably, this ardour failed to match the demands required for completion. Greed and incompetence denied success for thirty-four years, by which time the original promoters were dead.

Towards the end of 1792, the Gloucester Canal Committee made a decision. They invited Robert Mylne to take the necessary steps to obtain an Act of Parliament for their new canal. He arrived in Gloucester on 25th January 1793, stayed four days, on two of which he examined the preconceived line.

On 29th January, he went to Newent to examine Clowes' Gloucester and Hereford Canal

"and returned - chaise etc. to stand in lieu of maps bought for Gloucester Navigation. Made a report viva-voce - long and minute - 5 gns. Bills at Gloucester and Berkeley being paid by Mr. Comeline 15-7-0 expenses."[1]

Back in London, he set to work furiously. On 20th February, he "sent Mr Welles[2] long report and estimate of the Gloucester and Berkeley in a new method altered from the former and the three plans to be annexed thereto." A flurry of meetings and attendances at the Houses of Commons and Lords ensued. The Act was passed on 25th March. Three days later, Mylne "dined with the Gloucester Canal Committee - instructions given thereon."

A vital hurdle had been overcome in record time. His clients must have been delighted. Six months then passed while the Gloucester Canal Committee deliberated who to appoint their Chief Engineer.

This proved none too easy, for reputable engineers were scarce in 1793. In that one year, no less than thirty-two canal Enabling Acts were passed. Hadfield[3] has no doubt of the name first considered.

'Then came Jessop - alone - to tower over the period ... of the Canal mania ... in its wildest extent, from 1789 to 1796. Four engineers took the brunt; Robert Mylne and Robert Whitworth ... Jessop himself; and the younger John Rennie".[4]

In a table of involvement with Enabling Acts, Hadfield lists Jessop 27, Rennie 16, Whitworth 7, Mylne 6. This is only half the story as Mylne's journals, for the same period exactly, reveal Mylne as consultant for 27 canal projects admittedly often in opposition to them and not always required as a witness at the Houses of Parliament.

On the basis of his table, Hadfield infers that Mylne must have been considered a poor third, prompted perhaps by Mylne's later jibe at Jessop as a "Common Canal Cutter". But as Tony Conder, Curator of the National Waterways Museum at Gloucester observed "Charles Hadfield treats harshly anyone who gets at Jessop". [5]

So Mylne, Whitworth and Jessop were all invited "to survey the line in more detail" as a precursor to appointment as Chief Engineer. Even Clowes was asked to report "on such items as the most suitable place for brick works etc. along the line"[6] with a view, perhaps, to his appointment as Resident Engineer.

Whitworth declined the invitation, Jessop ignored it and Mylne accepted, and so returned to Gloucester on 15th September 1793 to report to the Committee on 18th September and remain there until 1st October. It proved a busy fortnight. He marked the line, took levels, measured the Cam feeder "and sounded [the] River [Severn]", went to Bristol and Cirencester and "dined with the Bristol [and Cirencester] Canal Company."

On 26th September, the Gloucester Canal Company asked him

> "to recapitulate the report he delivered in writing in January last introducing therein such additional remarks and alterations as his **more deliberate survey** had pointed out".

A few days later, he had been appointed officially the "Chief and Principal Engineer of the Gloucester Canal Company" to bring to fruition the most ambitious canal project ever, with the mandate that

> "he will prepare drawings, sections and modells [sic] of every part of the canal, the locks and the basons [sic] according to his **own directions** and in that manner in which he shall conceive will most effectually convey his idea of the **best mode** of forming and perfecting the canal in all its parts."

Mylne carried out this mandate impeccably. It never specified the degree of his personal attendance upon the works nor, alas, the quality of the Resident Engineer. Nor did it allow for the vagaries of the proprietors on the Committee, whom he was to castigate later.

These vagaries, in fact, scuppered the entire project in this, the first, stage. It was made clear to Mylne that the canal was fixed to that line drawn by Thomas Pinnell in 1792. The Committee also recommended that the Company issue a **ten per cent** - not five per cent as normal - dividend prior to trading.

As part of his re-survey before appointment, Mylne had been briefed to report on Grazebrook's Bristol and Cirencester Canal and its junction with the new Gloucester Canal between Saul and Berkeley. His adverse report outraged Grazebrook's Committee. Mylne had already made enemies. Grazebrook remarked pointedly that "he saw no reason to alter his project entirely to accommodate Mr Mylne and the Gloucester and Berkeley Canal Committee."

Now to the matter of the estimates of the cost of this unusual project. When first asked to obtain the Act of Parliament in 1793, Mylne had been presented with a fixed line and an estimate for a canal "not less than 15ft deep." On 20th February, he submitted "an estimate for the Gloucester and Berkeley in a **new method** altered from the former" of exactly £121,529-10s-4 pence a half penny. A month later this was incorporated within the Act as the cost of a canal **18ft deep** to ensure passage of "Vessels of 300 tons burthen with keels", with power to raise up to £137,000 with, however, penal conditions delaying acquisition of land over many years rather than immediately.

Canal historians have mocked Mylne ever since regarding this estimate. Hadfield accused him of careless surveying. Stimpson dismissed Mylne as "a distinguished architect and water supply engineer [with] little canal experience [who] failed to take inflation into account [and] underestimated the work, being unacquainted with canal construction."

The Weavers stated that "Mylne estimated the cost precisely at £121,329-10s-4 pence half penny[7] [sic], which proved as wildly inaccurate as did most 'exact estimates'." None of these versions are correct. But, in any case, a halfpenny (0.2p) had value in 1793. Even in 1826 the main contractor for the Canal submitted a claim for one month's extra "to boys driving the horses, 4 at 2/- [10p]: 8/- [40p]."

The point, missed here, is that estimates **at this stage** bore no relation to overall costs[8] and certainly not to capital, dwindling by issue of dividends. No historian has realised that this venture was doomed from the start by the incompetence of the Canal Committee.

As a gesture of involvement and optimism, Mylne became a £1,000 Shareholder immediately. This act alone soon convinced him of the folly of his commitment and reminded him of his strictures, several years back, of Grazebrook, Perry and the Thames and Severn Canal.

In spite of his grandiose title, his Canal Committee had no intention of allowing him to fulfill his mandate without interference for it, not he, chose the Resident Engineer.

Who, then, were the members of this Canal Committee? All Gloucester men and true, as listed;

1.	Thomas Weaver	Pin Merchant.
2.	Richard Chandler	Woolstapler.
3.	Richard Brown Cheston	Doctor.
4.	Charles Brandon Trye	Surgeon.
5.	William Fendall	Barrister and Banker.
6.	Edwin Jeynes	Mercer and Banker.
7.	Thomas Mee, Esq.	Gentleman.
8.	Giles Greenaway, Esq.	Gentleman.

They answered to the Canal Company and its shareholders who met twice yearly unless further meetings were required. Those who attended Company meetings dined together, all expenses paid. In 1793, these amounted to not less than £40 per dinner - no halfpennies there - and continued inexorably, no matter the attendance, the debts, the mortgage, the non-payment of operatives, the cessation of work and lack of income.

These general meetings, progressively ill-attended, were chaired sometimes, but rarely, by the Duke of Norfolk, and in his absence by Dr Lysons, a local man of repute. Ostensibly men of "ardour and enterprise" who had, after all, conceived this "undertaking of magnitude", none of them possessed much knowledge of water hydraulics nor of contractual procedure of manpower control or costs - above all costs. Nor had they any idea - such was their greed - of funding such a project.

There was one man, one man only, William Fendall of Matson, who comprehended what was involved and to him Mylne turned and stayed with regularly when all turned sour. Alas, not even Fendall could change the force of destiny in the face of the blind ignorance of his fellow committee members. Mylne, in accepting his appointment as "Chief and Principal Engineer" had made the mistake of his career.

At least Mylne carried out his part of the mandate by submitting detailed drawings and specifications, together with models of bridges and pump engines. Indeed he provided a longitudinal section of the entire line. Only those of the lock, the double lock, from the Gloucester basin have survived (plates 17, 18) He even designed the Bridgemen's cottages - since attributed to Telford - in his inimitable neoclassical style.

The rub began with the appointment of the Resident Engineer. Of the candidates, two were short-listed. It must be remembered that in 1793 so many canals were being projected and empowered that any engineer of experience had already been engaged, so the field was sparse. Add to this the risible salary offered by the Canal Company and it is no wonder the quality of applicant proved questionable.

George Pinkerton and Denis Edson were the candidates, perhaps the only ones. The former was the nephew of John Pinkerton, Jessop's partner in canal construction who went bankrupt over the Dudley Tunnel. Even Jessop, approached for a testimonial, found difficulty in recommending him so he was rejected. That left Denis Edson.

He had advertised, without any qualifications, in the Bristol Journal dated 1st December 1792 as an "Engineer and Architect".

"Canal Navigations etc. Every branch of engineering and surveying is estimated and executed on eligible [sic] terms."[9]

In September 1794, on instructions from his committee, John Wheeler, Clerk of the Canal Company, engaged Denis Edson as Resident Engineer at £200 per annum[10] whereas Josiah Clowes had been appointed similarly to the Thames and Severn at £300 per annum a decade earlier. This appointment took nearly a year to ratify, by which time work on the canal had started. It proved disastrous.

Edson was not only incompetent, for he never measured work done nor quantity of materials used, but proved a rogue likewise. Even the Canal Committee had to accept his shortcomings, yet he was not dismissed until June 1795 by which time events had gone from bad to worse.

For the remainder of 1793 Mylne, had little time to even consider the duties of his new appointment so busy was he on the London Canal and the problems of the Ouse outfall at King's Lynn, yet somehow or other he found time to prepare drawings.

In January 1794 two important Gloucester men, Mr Cambridge and Mr Fendall were in London. Mylne "waited" on the former to discuss "his Mills and Lands for the Gloucester Canal and various parts of his works - long and tedious." Mr Cambridge, the most vital landowner on the Canal line could make or break the project. He owned Cambridge Village and the Cam streams that join the Severn at Frampton Pill. These streams were required as the primary water feeder to the Canal. Eventually this feeder became a branch narrowboat cut to a coal wharf at Cambridge.

Three days later, on 8th February, Mr Fendall of Matson called on Mylne for "long explanations and descriptions of the drawings of the Gloucester Canal". Later that month Mylne spent "all day at work on the Gloucester Canal estimates" which were despatched early in February, together with "a long letter on fire engines" (i.e. water pumps).

Meanwhile, in the absence of a Resident Engineer, William Crosley had been commissioned to retake levels and check those by Pinnell and Hall and "by Clewes [sic] on the first conceived line."[11] Mylne intended to present a report with drawings and estimates based on Crosley's levels at the Gloucester Canal Company General Meeting on 31st March 1794, "but he ... [was] ... unfortunately called to attend the House of Lords on the Rochdale Canal Bill the day before." This valid excuse did not prevent a resolution being passed desiring him "to come to Gloucester to expedite the start of work."

For this same meeting Mylne had noted in his Business Journal for 19th March "Gave Mr Triart [sic] drawing of a digging machine for the Gloucester and Berkeley Canal - to set a model thereof."

For two years the relationship between Committee and Chief Engineer proved cordial with recorded minutes extolling Mylne's virtues and the foresight in appointing him. This changed inexorably to a permanent grumble of exasperation, after which the storm broke, with Trye and Lysons[12] as thunder and lightning.

At this stage Mylne, unaware of the impending storm, left London on 5th June 1794 for Gloucester, via Abingdon where he examined the Upper Thames, the Thames and Severn Canal to Whitminster - the proposed junction with his Canal - and thence along the line to Gloucester. There, four days later, he attended an "irregular" meeting of his committee "the whole day - dined together - went and examined Mr Trye's machine."

He then "set out the figure of the new Bason [sic] - the island, streets etc. ... and wharf". The original scheme had shown a hexagonal basin but Mylne altered this to a more modest size at this stage whilst retaining the angle for the north wall and, with a view to further extension, left the east boundary a grassed slope. He sensed already the financial stricture to come.

He then walked the line, yet again, making a detour to Sharpness Point indicative of dissatisfaction with the fixed line to Berkeley Pill. On 13th June he invited his Committee to breakfast before taking members along the entire line, paying particular attention to the proposed junction with the Stroudwater Canal above Whitminster Lock as planned. This he considered ill-conceived, resulting in extra cutting of the entire main line level, and advised a junction below the lock.

To those such as Trye this amounted to unwelcome and adverse criticism of their original conception, yet made sense to William Fendall who realised by now that Mylne knew his business and was prone to speak his mind bluntly. This he did in reports to the Committee on 16th June, and again on 17th, after which he returned to London.

Back again, early in August, he spent a week conferring with Grazebrook about the Bristol and Cirencester project and killed it to the latter's dismay and grievance. Grazebrook must surely have been a shareholder of the Gloucester Canal and as such joined the clique which later obtained Mylne's dismissal as Chief Engineer. But this is supposition.

In September 1794 Mylne "sent Mr Wheeler [an] advertisement and three long particulars for digging the canal - the Mason work and Brickwork - very long and minute with form of proposals for each." This was for the tenderers of the work to ensure understanding of what was involved in this huge and novel task. They were required to cut a specimen length of line before submitting a tender; a wise precaution.

Between 18th and 29th October 1794 Mylne was again at Gloucester, meeting his Committee and advancing the project, in accordance with his reports of June that year, in which he submitted his revised estimate of £121,529 together with a list of items **extra** to this total.

1.	22 Swing Bridges for roads and four similar at the Basins at an average of £300 each.	£7,800
2.	Emptying the cut ... by movable fire engine during the work, cross dams, use of boats to move the soil.	£1,500
3.	Ten acres of lands at Gloucester to form a bason, pound, locks wharfs and Quays, new roads etc.	£1,140
4.	Expense of forming roads or ways into streets at Gloucester.	£1,000
5.	Levelling a considerable space of land at the termination of the Canal and making a bason therein for the demurrage of large vessels waiting for proper tides, wind and weather etc.	£1,000
6.	Unforeseen accidents, extra cost on some of these articles, low charges, superintendence of works at ten percent[13]	£11,029

Mylne also presented a new section of the canal, taken longitudinally along the entire length with twenty-five cross-sections, "at different and most essential parts of it" together with a treatise on "wet Docks, Quays and Warehouses."

The day after this marathon meeting, Mylne conferred with the County Magistrates "on the proper plan and disposition of the streets, wharfs [sic] etc. contiguous to the County Gaol" and discussed public footways and the extent of the gaol in relation to the basin and wharves. Few contemporary engineers could match such assiduity.

The September invitation to tender for excavation was won by William Montague - a friend of Trye - at a rate of 5d per yard - "tools, plants, wheelbarrows, machines etc. all found." In spite of the demonstration cut prior to tender, Montague, like other contractors, soon opted out.

At the Committee meeting that month the members resolved, and duly minuted, "to give a fair trial to the machine invented by Mr Trye, without further risk or expense to the Company." Shortly after a model of a machine for driving piles, submitted by Mylne, was approved, he being "requested to procure such a machine of proper size to be executed when necessary." [14]

In the autumn of 1794, trial holes were dug within the basin area to find suitable earth for brickmaking and all was ready to cut the first length of Canal to Hempsted. At the General Meeting on 27th October tribute was made to the Chief Engineer, in his presence, that "no public work of this kind has ever been better furnished with papers to proceed with than have been produced with his industry."

And so the great undertaking began. Setbacks came early in profusion.

Floods prevented the staking out of the wharf. In fact the weather, over the first five months, proved so inclement "as to preclude the possibility of any active exertion". One of the contractors for the basin died of consumption shortly after starting and Edson, the Resident Engineer, soon revealed his incompetence. Late in February 1795, Mylne received the usual summons;

> "In consequence of a report from Mr Edson ... respecting the impracticability of depositing the earth within the distance mentioned in your letter to him, and also of the necessity of pudling [sic] that part ... which Mr Montague has contracted for, it is ... (the committee's) ... very earnest wish that you contrive to come to Gloucester as soon as possible ...".

Mylne's position was fast becoming untenable. Events began to move towards an inevitable crisis. Edson had to be restrained from signing contracts on his own initiative and his conduct was so unsatisfactory that in June 1795 he was dismissed, whereupon he wrote a scurrilous letter to the committee, abusing his principal. After he had gone, it was discovered that he had issued faulty instructions and neglected to measure the work already done. Edson even had the impudence to offer "to contract for cutting a portion of the line ... from Pegthorne Hill", an offer which was, of course, rejected out of hand. Edson, clearly, was more "canal cutter" than engineer.

The Committee than engaged James Dadford[15] to replace Edson, but on a yearly basis. The Dadfords had a reputation of sorts for Thomas, senior, was involved with Brindley on the Stafford and Worcester and the Trent and Mersey Canals ostensibly as a surveyor and engineer. His son Thomas, junior, was "a good theoretical engineer, known for his work on Welsh Canals, but was eventually dismissed ... due to inattention at work and inability to control workmen." (Gladwin and White.) It would appear that James Dadford was nephew of Thomas, senior and when appointed Resident Engineer to the Gloucester Canal was but twenty-six and totally inexperienced.

The early enthusiasm shown by the committee was evaporating fast, the initial ardour giving way to a sullen caution that betrayed financial anxiety, yet dividends were still being paid out. The Committee manifested its worries to Mylne in a letter in which he was again summoned to Gloucester "as there are certain points of very material consequence contained in your plans and directions which are not satisfactory"[16]. The clerk wrote that the Committee members were "so very anxious to have doubts removed, that much embarrassed them, and **as they conceive very much affect their future operations**, that they cannot be satisfied, but by your personal attendance, which they trust you will not defer longer than one week."

Mylne rarely refused such summons. Indeed in 1795 he travelled to Gloucester six times staying there for up to a week on each visit. On those in March and May he made a point of dining (i.e. lunching) personally with several members of the Canal Committee and likewise with several shareholders, Dr Lyson included, as well as Comeline, the Company solicitor.[17]

As the summer of 1795 reached its zenith, the excavation of the basin[18] progressed albeit George Milne, contractor, replaced Thomas Baker who was unable to fulfil his contract. The first section of the cut along the south side of Hempsted had also progressed favourably, in the charge of George Mills, when Mylne arrived in Gloucester on August 21st to attend a meeting of the committee. At this meeting he propounded the principles on which the basin was being laid out and the manner in which he intended to construct the wharves. Before adjournment, he was **instructed** to prepare comparative estimates of the costs of continuing the wharf walls to the bottom of the basin excavation or taking them down to the half-way mark. He received instructions also to embark upon the erection of the first bridge. On his next visit in September he submitted for the Committee's approval "a set of drawings and a model forming a design for the Swing Bridges proposed to be made across the canal; Whereupon ... it was resolved that the same should serve as a pattern for all the road bridges upon the canal." It appears that Telford was sufficiently satisfied with these twenty years later to adopt the pattern along the whole line.

It was in September too that James Dadford finally arrived in Gloucester to replace Edson. Now Dadford's uncle, Thomas senior, had been elected a member of The Smeatonian Society as long ago as 1783 and was therefore known to Mylne. Perhaps as a test, Mylne immediately required Dadford to check Crosley's levels along the line; "the difference proved to be 3 inches."

In view of later strictures by historians of careless surveying, this enigmatic journal note possibly assumes considerable importance concerning Dadford's ability as surveyor and appointed Resident Engineer. A difference of 3" between Crosley's and Dadford's figures appears slight, so why did Mylne note it?

When translated into cubic capacity of canal cutting, earth disposal, payment rates for labour and filling with water the widest and deepest canal ever attempted, the situation is altered radically even over a length of a mere 17 and three quarter miles. In water capacity alone, the difference involves some extra thirteen million gallons of water – no minor consideration nor cost.

Clearly Mylne's odd entry in his Business Journal was a record and reminder of Dadford's inexperience and frailty. It is to his credit, or rashness, that he failed to use it later, when Dadford was extolled at Mylne's expense, to defend himself against his detractors, at the time of his dismissal. But then Mylne's integrity would deny such action.

The Committee had provided Mylne with a dwelling alongside workshops on the Severn Ait, north of the basin opposite the County Gaol. Although he did make use of this occasionally, he preferred to stay with William Fendall at the latter's home at Matson outside the City. Fendall, barrister and banker, was a member of the Canal Company Committee and it is conceivable that the ensuing drama stemmed as much from incompatibility between Fendall and Trye as it did between Trye and Mylne.

In their many overnight discussions, Mylne and Fendall must have considered the finance of the project and the implications of dividends issued, without income return, since March 1793. Both Banker and Chief Engineer realised the inevitable consequences of such idiocy, yet they were powerless to convince Trye, Lysons and others of impending disaster.

NOTES

1.	Mylne's Business Journals.
2.	Clerk to the Canal Company.
3.	William Jessop. Hadfield and Skempton. 1979 David and Charles.
4.	Ibid. 3.
5.	Letter Conder to Author. 7th July 1992.
6.	M. Stimpson. History of Gloucester Docks. 1980.
7.	Gloucester and Sharpness Canal. C.P. and C.R. Weaver. c.1950.
8.	Mylne completed Blackfriars Bridge in 1769 for £163 less than his original estimate in 1760.
9.	Canal Builders. Anthony Burton. Eyre Methuen. 1972.
10.	Evidence of lack of qualifications or parsimony by the Canal Company.
11	The Crosley Family

   a)	William Crosley Snr. Resident Engineer under Rennie and Jessop for the Rochdale Canal. Died late in 1796. That Crosley had to travel from Rochdale to Gloucester is some measure of the scarcity of reputable surveyors during the Canal Mania.

   b)	William Crosley Jnr. Last Resident Engineer on Rochdale Canal, 1802-1804. Last Resident Engineer on Lancaster Canal under Rennie, 1817-1819.

12.	The Lysons Family

   12.1	Dr Daniel Lysons (1727-1800) Physician MA Oxon., Fellow All Souls, MD. Published medical works. Of Hempsted Court, Gloucester.

   12.2	Rev. Daniel Lysons (1762-1834) MA Oxon. Nephew of the above. Held family living at Rodmarton, Glos. 1804-1833. Topographer. Principal work "Environs of London" 1792-6. With brother Samuel compiled "Magna Britannia - Account of the Counties of Great Britain" - ten Counties, Bedfordshire to Devonshire, alphabetically 1806-22. Also published - 1800 - "An Historical Account of those Parishes in the County of Middlesex which are not described in the environs of London."

   12.3	Samuel Lysons (1763-1819). Antiquary, FSA, FRS, Barrister, Keeper of Tower of London Records 1803. Vice-president and Treasurer Royal Society 1810. Antiquary Professor, Royal Academy 1818. Assisted brother Daniel on "Magna Britannia". Greatest work :'Reliquiae Britannico Romanae' published 1801-1817.

   12.4	Dr Lysons' niece, Mary, sister to Daniel and Samuel Lysons, married in 1792 Charles Brandon Trye. There can be little or no doubt that Dr Lysons relied upon his nephew, Daniel, the topographer, to fix the line of the Gloucester and Berkeley Canal after Clowes' initial survey. Equally, the Rev. Daniel must have met Jessop on the Grand Junction Canal when preparing one or other of his books and maybe even earlier in conjunction with 'Magna Britannia' when Jessop was involved with the Basingstoke Canal.

   On the feasible assumption that Jessop and Mylne were antipathetic, the Lysons/Trye clique can be associated justifiably with Jessop and the Pinkertons without hint of intended impropriety. It is just that Lysons and Trye, both medics, claimed pseudo-expertise in engineering and used this to attack Mylne and defend Dadford, their choice as Resident Engineer.

13.	This 10% poses a problem, for it refers neither to the extras nor to the total estimate.
14.	The Times reported in August 1796 a machine used on the Gloucester and Berkeley Canal on a conveyor-belt principle with barrows hauled in a continuous chain so that with only two men 1,400 barrow loads were shifted on a 40ft run in 12 hours. This is evidence of Mylne's inventiveness.
15	The Dadford Family
	Tony Conder, Curator - National Waterways Museum, Gloucester, letter to the author, 1992: "John Dadford was brother to Thomas Jnr, both being sons of Thomas Snr. John worked on

the Neath and the Montgomery, either sharing or passing on work to the family. John moved to America in 1797. James Dadford is presumed to be a younger brother to the other two, but information is sketchy."

16. This ambiguous statement suggests that the Committee could not read Mylne's detailed drawings or, alternatively, wanted alterations which they dared not make for lack of expertise. It could also have been the start of the conspiracy that followed to oust Mylne. At this stage, there was NO Resident Engineer.

17. This was far in excess of the recognised duties of a Consultant or Chief Engineer at that time.

18. Committee minutes record "ordered that Mr Wheeler pay the workmen who found the coins one guinea (£1-1-0) and that he count them over and deliver them to Mr Cheston, who has kindly offered to decypher them, and give his opinion of their value."

Not to the finders, be it noted, but to the committee which represented the canal Company, the owners of the land. To have paid one guinea in 1793 indicated the importance of the cache.

4

THE CONSPIRACY

"What poor things mortals can become when the seat of reason is knocked awry
by animus, spite and bigotry."

(Joseph Holloway)

Dr Daniel Lysons owned Hempsted Court, a property that embraced most of the land around the village of Hempsted occupying the only high ground between Gloucester and the Severn, a mile to the south-west of the town. A shareholder in the canal company, he proved totally intractable over a certain matter which, in Mylne's view, was vital to the finances of the project. In the later report in defence of his conduct, presented in January of 1796, Mylne wrote:

> "No persuasion could have any effect upon Dr Lysons and **his friends** to allow the line of the canal to pass on the west side of Hempsted Hill where there would have been no deep cutting at all, causing thereby a great expense to be incurred by you on the present line ... in addition thereto ... the soil dug out of the deep part of the deep cutting must **not** be laid on the banks of the Canal in the Avenue part of that estate."[1]

Lysons's niece, Mary, married, in 1792, Charles Brandon Trye FRS, senior surgeon of the Gloucester Infirmary. A local man, his family had owned Hardwicke Court, an extensive property bordering the Roman Road, five miles south of Gloucester. This, the family had sold recently to Earl Hardwicke who adopted the name for his title. Born in 1757, Trye had been apprenticed to a Worcester apothecary in 1773. After two years in London he was appointed Medical Officer in 1780 to the Infirmary in Gloucester where he lived thereafter. In 1797, he inherited a cousin's estate at Leckhampton Hill which he developed as a stone quarry served by a branch tramroad, constructed 1806-1811, for coal transported via the Severn and Gloucester Docks. Trye died, aged 57, in 1811, the same year as Mylne.

Trye, an energetic member of the Canal Committee, was among those Mylne termed as "Dr Lysons's friends". They fell out early on, in January 1794, when "Mr Trye presented a modell [sic] of a machine invented by himself for removing earth" to his colleagues on the Committee. A prototype was duly ordered and, as Mylne suspected, "proved useless", whereas the "Fire engine [i.e. water pump] constructed according to the descriptions given by Mr Mylne" in the workshops of Messrs. Boulton and Watt, after a faulty start due to misuse, functioned efficiently under Mylne's personal supervision.

"Proved useless" - Mylne's own term[2] - could not have endeared him to Trye who recalled Mylne's two reports to the Committee the previous year, at the time he staked out the boundary of the basin. The first dealt with the methods of construction Mylne intended to employ. He had urged the digging of a small cutter canal, 20 feet broad by 4 foot 6 inches deep, to enable cheap and rapid carriage of materials and labour forces. He recommended that the section from Gloucester to the Stroud Canal be constructed first, an obviously sound proposition for then boats could load at the canal mouth at Framilode on the Severn and at the junction, near Saul, change onto the new cut and ply up to Gloucester, thus creating an immediate return on the capital expenditure. Mylne also stressed the **necessity for the purchase of all land** through which the canal was to be cut **before operations began.** He closed this report by pointing out that as "the Bason and locks at Gloucester and the intended aqueduct at the Stroud are rather of an intricate and unusual nature for most men's comprehension ... models of both should be made by which means workmen and your agents would understand in a better degree, the end and purpose they are to work upon."

In the second report Mylne dismissed the line of the collateral cut to Berkeley Town as "extremely ill-laid out and injudiciously conceived" especially as regards the height of the main street of the town above the wharf, proposing in its place a new line with a square basin, off to one side, reached by means of the road below the town, thus avoiding much cutting and relaying of sewers. He discussed the disadvantages that would result from acceding to Lord Berkeley's wish that the line should be clear of Branwood, and wound up with an analysis of the shoals and fisheries in the Severn opposite the Pill mouth.

Such bluntness, such criticism of the project, however correct, however justified, proved offensive to those who had conceived it. And Trye had been foremost in this.

Meanwhile it had been arranged from the start for the company to manufacture its own brick supply from earth near the basin, but not long after commencement, Mr Brassington the brick-maker, obtained permission to utilise the earth within the basin. Whether this affected the bricks materially or not is irrelevant. The bricks were unfit for use and brick-making, consequently, was halted. The deficiency had to be relieved by a bulk purchase of some millions of bricks from the Herefordshire and Gloucestershire Canal Company. This unforeseen extra caused a furore for already money was short because capital had been squandered on dividends rather than construction. It goaded the dissidents to action. They submitted an insinuating paper of queries designed to sow doubt in the minds of the shareholders to persuade them, when the time came, to distrust the ability of their Chief Engineer and so obtain his dismissal.

Charles Trye was entrusted with the first tilt at Mylne and, in November 1795, he concocted "a paper of calculations on certain parts of the canal ... relating to the banks and towing paths thereof." Naturally, this was done in Mylne's absence. On 30th December he met the Committee to explain his actions. This he did forcibly at a Special General Meeting.

Trye had picked Mylne's estimates to pieces. He stressed his use of faulty land values and maintained there were errors in computation as well as omissions. Mylne replied that outright acquisition "of land on the line" was essential and economical in the long run. He further pointed out that "the design for this undertaking went into Parliament with an estimated cost of £137,238 and came out with a variety of loads upon it, not conceived at first and quite **unprecedented** in any Canal Act hitherto. It is now well-known [he continued] the demand of thirty-eight years purchase [of land] inserted in the Act was made to overset the scheme entirely and this turns out to be ten or twelve years purchase too much, in **my opinion**, as **the value of land and money** is at this **present time**." Demolishing Trye's contentions one by one, Mylne was unable to resist the opportunity to fight back and, changing to the offensive, - one can picture him commanding the attention of the assembly with his aquiline nose, determined chin thrust out defiantly and eyes agleam with mischief - he ended thus;

> "having gone through the particulars of this paper I shall say generally; that Gentlemen who make observations and animadversions on works, and papers constructed for their execution, should do it in the same line of the original papers; state their data; and construct their papers in the spirit of and consonant to the original on which they are inquisitive and mean them to be compared in the result."

These words were similar to those made to the proprietors of the Thames and Severn Canal two years previously when asked to report on the deficiencies of their Canal.

Trye was not the sole antagonist; Mr Stock had compiled a paper on costs. Mylne countered this by reminding shareholders that there was a war on and that due to rising prices "the present situation might not be wondered at." Mylne contended that the requests by contractors for various increased rates should be viewed sympathetically as their original tenders

> "might be a little out on that head, as there is no canal of eighteen feet general depth which has yet been cut in this or any other country [besides which] You have had the great misfortune of **placing a person** to set out these men's work in so slow, ignorant and inaccurate a manner that it has an inconceivable influence against reasonable prices; [he was, of course, referring to Edson] no ready measurements of quantities done every Saturday could be obtained from his stupidity and obstinacy ... decisive measures and regular pay are the great means of lessening the price of this labour which in this undertaking is **one half of the whole expense**"

After answering Mr Stock fully, Mylne then presented a report "on the general mode of executing the Canal with a full and compleat [sic] estimate of all expenses." He shocked them from the start by declaring that completion of the canal including **ALL** expenses would now cost £169,440-8s-9 pence half penny.

"In making out this prospective view of your affairs" [he informed his audience] "I have done nothing professionally but the estimate of the purchases [i.e. land] **to be made** and works **to be done** - all the other articles are those which make **no part** of an Engineer's consideration [i.e. administration, salaries, company expenses and professional fees] but as it is necessary to be done by **some person** before you can possibly have a correct view of the whole and the effect produced ... I thought I could not do a better service to the undertaking than giving a statement that would prove the zeal, if not the ability, of a friend and a proprietor [i.e. shareholder].

No less than seven different estimates of the **like kind** have been made since the first time this scheme was agitated in 1792 and they have varied according to the **variation of the scheme** itself and the information collected from quarters most to be relied upon.

[He lists all seven - the first two by Clowes]

1.	£102,108	(Land £40)
2.	£140,852	(—·— £80)
3.	£137,238	(—·— £50)
4.	£139,988	(—·— £50)
5.	£126,504	(—·— £38)
6.	£121,329	(—·— £38)
7.	£126,000	(—·— £40)

I have in two separate papers ... endeavoured to show that **a tardy method** of performing a vigorous measure creates expense and increases prices, which otherwise would be comparatively low and more reasonable.

[He blames] an order for dividends to be paid on each subscriber's original capital investment for depletion of the sum needed to the completion of this great work [adding that] up to this date **£6,829** had been paid out for **work done.**

The whole scheme is only a **machine** and if there is one peg wanting in it a little while before it is finished the whole capital invested lays idle for the time as to its being productive while the interest [i.e. dividends] is devouring the substance and enlarging the capital [expenditure]. This circumstance alone has rendered many schemes of canals abortive though they were good plans in themselves at first setting off. Under the pressure and influence of this idea I have constantly pressed for more speedy measures and proposed different modes of proceeding with the works which would bring the whole to a close at some particular time.

[On labour costs, Mylne observed that] when the present scarcity of labourers throughout the whole country occasioned by the unexampled armies and fleets of the present war and the present price of provisions, far exceeding any former times, are considered, and that these [problems] have begun to operate since the first estimate ... of 1793 the present situation is not to be wondered at.

Decisive measures and regular pay are the great means of lessening the price of this labour which in this undertaking is one half of the whole expense. There is not enough competition either [besides which] additional contracts were delayed unaccountably."

He mentioned the slow methods of working, suggested ways of improvement and proposed a larger labour force split up so that cutting might be performed from both ends of the line as well as both ways from the junction at Saul.

Mylne then reminded the meeting of his original and still favoured idea of a preliminary feeder canal some eight or nine feet deep to be enlarged at some later date. This would produce immediate revenue besides quickening the work on the major scheme. After this spirited effort, Mylne dined the following day with the Committee and "Supp't at home with Mr Dadford." He returned to London on January 10th 1796.

Mylne has been pilloried relentlessly for his estimates.

"My only recollection of Mylne's work on the Gloucester and Sharpness Canal" states Brian Dice, Chief Executive of British Waterways (letter to the author) "is that he was dismissed because his costings were incompetent. Perhaps you will be able to vindicate him."

The crucial point here is why were no less than seven estimates required by the Committee betweeb 1792 and 1795. As Mylne declares, "they varied according to the variation of the scheme itself." In modern parlance, "The goal-posts had been moved."

Take those by Clowes for instance. Even with land value doubled between the two, it is clear that a variation of line caused the major increase in costs for the second estimate. This suggests that Sharpness had been his original choice of terminus. Mylne's estimate (N⁰· 7) on a like land value reflects the switch to the Berkeley terminus at an extra cost of £24,892 - an increase of twenty percent - always remembering these were construction costs **plus** dividend payments.

At the September General Meeting in 1796, less than a month after the attempt by Lysons and Trye to obtain his dismissal, Mylne's advice was translated into a curious resolution to finish the canal quickly

> **"to stop the drain of money because no adequate recompense [sic] can be expected to accrue to the Proprietors, for the money advanced by them, until the entire completion of the Canal."**

It proved a Pyrrhic victory for both Mylne and for the Company as seven months later, Wheeler the Clerk to the Company, reported

> "In the afternoon of the 6th [May] while I was paying the day men, James Wilkins, the holder of the last mentioned draft for £110 came to me and said 'they will not pay this note - they say they have no effects - they have but about £12 in their hands.' I replied 'take it to Mr Jelf(e)'."

Whence then had the original capital disappeared? This had amounted to over £200,000 in 1793. By January 1796 under £7000 had been spent on the work itself and, when this finally ceased in 1799, the alleged total allocated to work completed was said to be £100,000. Where had the other half gone other than on dividends and Company expenses?

Why, for instance, had it been necessary to obtain a further Act of Parliament in 1795? One reason was to vary the line[3],another to raise more money, but why?

Mylne makes no mention of this in his Business Journals but the Canal Company received a letter dated 8th December 1796 from John Blackburn of London declining to become a subscriber as "Mr Mylne being employed as the Surveyor is almost an insurmountable objection as I have experienced his unpleasant temper and tyrannical conduct on many occasions."[4] How true was this?

Clearly Mylne's bluntness raised hackles, including those of Dr Lysons who now entered the fray by trying to force the Canal Committee to dismiss Mylne. In a cautious reply, the Committee replied that "as the ... work is now going on ... [and the] ... next General Meeting is so near at hand, they think it not advisable immediately to direct a new survey or employ another Engineer." The Doctor returned to the attack by claiming that a Mr Jordan of Oakhill had invented an improved bridge which should be considered and that a Surveyor of his own choice, Mr Symonds of Goswell Street, London, would "wait upon the Committee".

Lysons, it seems, not only questioned Mylne's swing bridge design but his levels too, and to this end demanded a special General Meeting.

This was convened on 6th January 1796. Mylne attended and delivered a long and detailed report in which he stated forcibly that "there were points settled before I had the honour of being consulted" the principal one being that of "the correspondence which the level of this Canal must have with a certain part of the Stroud Canal and the impossibility of changing the line of situation at that place has given a general cast to the **whole mode of executing** the Canal."

Mylne had made this point before and, on the plan for the 1795 Act, had marked possible deviations from the original line in agreement with William Fendall and others. Just prior to this meeting he had noted "setting out the **middle** line" and three days later "the **central** line", together with an enigmatic entry "went on line beyond Hempsted Hill to

Dr Lysons for a house - and more land."

Mylne concluded that Pinnell's original junction with the Stroudwater Canal ABOVE Whitminster (Wheatenhurst) lock was totally impractical and must be made on the pound below, several feet down to reduce excavation and cost, even if this meant raising the level of the pound and the provision of an extra lock on the Stroudwater below the junction. He was, of course, proved right.

Aware too of the rapid dissipation of capital by dividend issues, Mylne had, as a temporary measure, reduced the size of the Gloucester basin and at the same time increased his estimate in spite of claims that the deviations would reduce costs. His critics, stung by his bluntness, turned to finding fault with his detailed drawings of all aspects of construction.

At the next General Meeting, on 28th March 1796, Dr Lysons took the chair. Both Mylne and Edson were present. After thanking Mr Trye and Mr Stock for their papers "which should be remembered as work proceeds" Dr Lysons directed that a resolution be proposed that due to

> "many of the Proprietors entertaining doubts whether some improvements might not be made to the present plan of executing the Canal ... two able engineers be called in to ... give their opinions whether any or what improvements could be made, [and] that Mr Jessop and Mr Whitworth be applied to, to survey the line [and] ... failing them, Mr Sheasby."

The resolution was carried.

Two days following this meeting, Mylne laid out the lines of the basin and set out the new bridge and the roads converging upon it. On April 2nd he "attended Mr Whitworth at the office [and] explained the plan and execution" and then, in company with Dadford, they inspected work in progress, continuing down the line to Hardwicke. The three then dined at the King's Head. The foundation stone of the quay wall to the basin was laid on April 4th, but on the 13th the Committee "received Mr Whitworth's observations upon the quay wall ... and a plan for a [new] wall." As a result, instructions were issued to stop all work on the basin until further notice.

Early the next month Jessop, surprisingly available, accompanied Mylne to Gloucester where together they inspected the line to enable Jessop to prepare his report which he made to the Committee, viva voce, with Mylne present, on 16th May promising a written one early the next month. Not until 27th July were both his and Whitworth's received. Meanwhile Mylne had, as he himself noted, "bored 24ft below the basin." In view of what transpired, this is important.

> 'The earliest Drawing ... is one headed 'Mr Mylns [sic] Locks at Gloucester 1793' [which] indicates quay walls with footings at 16ft, a water depth of 13ft adjacent to the quays and a depth of 18ft in the basin."[5] (Plate 17)

Trye and his companions now felt justified in showing their hand in a bid to oust Mylne, on the strength of these two outside reports. They convened a Special General Meeting for 15th August 1796. Because Trye monopolised the whole time, the bid nearly succeeded. He had arranged for two letters to be read out, one written by himself, the other by Edmund Stock. These were followed by the reports of Jessop and Whitworth, after which Trye delivered his attack on Mylne, which - as planned by the dissidents - was to culminate in a vote for his dismissal. The ruse failed.

Trye's letter dated 4th April was brief and simply recorded his protests against the foundations of the Wharf wall on the west side of the basin being "laid upon the bench of earth instead of ... **below** the bottom of the bason." Stock's letter, also, dealt with this point and was dated 20th April.

> "It must be obvious," he wrote "to everyone when he [Whitworth] saw the work upon the bason was prosecuting and might be far advanced before Mr Jessop and himself could meet; and upon a plan evidently wrong, it was necessary he should give his opinion upon that particular part of the work ... to prevent the folly — the folly and expense of putting up and pulling down. **I MAY BE CALLED OFFICIOUS ... BUT ...** I have a right to give my sentiments. My opinion is that the committee, having proceeded upon the bason (which perhaps is the most objectionable part of the undertaking) after a vote of the

last General Meeting, have taken upon themselves a responsibility which they have often declared against. [Stock ended upon a note of humbug.] I trust you will acquit me of every other motive but the general good, and not impute my interference to causes which **I detest and abhor**."

To Trye and his confederates, the two reports by the engineers were hardly satisfactory. Whitworth was under the misapprehension that it was to have been a joint report and that, had he known separate reports were desired before he traversed the line, he would be better equipped to answer the queries now set him. "I do not think I can ... without seeing the country" he pleaded, adding that he was now busy on the "Grand Commercial Canal," but "I find Mr Jessop agrees with me about the section of the wharf wall." In this he was incorrect and proved a little anticipatory, however, as we shall see. Meanwhile, he appended a short description of how he thought the wharf wall should be constructed of piling, limestone and ashlar, not ashlar backed by bricks only. He had found time to review the general plan and line as fixed by Mylne and objected to little and praised a great deal. In fact, he and Jessop, in accord with the scheme as a whole, differed only on the Wharf wall.

Jessop declared "Gloucester Bason could do **without walls if necessary** but if the maximum space is needed, no better method than Mr Whitworth's [suggestion]; the mode by Mr Mylne is the middle way, **a half wall on a bench would be at least as permanent as a wall of the whole height and might be half the expense** ... but some wharf room would be lost. **Both ways are safe** ... I think turning bridges more convenient than drawbridges." This opinion reversed that of Whitworth's. Jessop did maintain that passing places for ships were desirable.

Trye, unperturbed by this lack of firm support, "delivered to the meeting the following observations." Nine of these were petty but the final one formed the mainspring of his attack.

"I represented the estimate (called the Improved Estimate) as extremely inaccurate and deficient ... as it was the cause of the **present deficiency in shares held by the Proprietors and may give rise to all the evils to be expected from our finances being unequal to the important work which we have undertaken**.[6] [He reminded the committee that he had] repeatedly, repeatedly and repeatedly stated the defects in the scheme [as he saw them] and that the rectitude of these [opinions] ... may be proved by the works already done, by the clear, decided, methodical and judicious replies of Mr Whitworth ... and by the **inferences** that can be drawn from Mr Jessop's compendious report; and these opinions may be contrasted with Mr Mylne's by a reference to his reports, plans, specifications and letters to the Committee **and to the Resident Engineer**. I have entertained doubts as to the propriety of several others of his proceedings; some of these have been submitted to Messrs. Whitworth and Jessop ... Mr Whitworth's answers show that these doubts were entertained on the best grounds ... it must now, I believe, be universally admitted that I have not idly or wantonly excited the attention ... of the Proprietors."

The unctuous references to Whitworth and the cunning allusion to Jessop's "inferences" could hardly have passed unnoticed by a number of the shareholders; and when "further observations" were made by Messrs. Stock, Lysons, Coles and Croombe, the more discerning must have sensed an atmosphere, or rather an undercurrent, of malevolence, exuded by this group towards Mylne, the object of their impeachment.

He, it appears, disdained any allusion to this personal attack, confining himself in his reply to dealing with the allegations against his methods and to answering the "observations".

The vote of confidence was then taken. The result afforded little jubilation to either party for, as Mylne recorded, "Vote on me – 205 against; 252 for."

* * * * *

During 1796, Company records list two sets of contractors; that for April in detail, the other in December less so. Comparison indicates the state of Company funds which, in May the following year, reached a nadir.

APRIL 1796

Thomas Baker	-	Bason at Gloucester.
Humphrey Brown	-	Water carriage of stone.
Dennis Edson	-	Engaged as Engineer.
Homfray and Co	-	Cast Iron pipes.
Peter James	-	Building the stage.
Sampson Lockstone	-	Bason at Gloucester.
Ditto	-	Part of the Canal.
William Montague	-	Forming Canal.
George Mills	-	Canal digger.
James Pinkerton	-	ditto (Missing)
Stroud and Co	-	Brickwork and Stonework.
John Pixton	-	Canal Cutter.
Richard Sayer	-	Brickmaker.
George Milne	-	Bason work.

DECEMBER 1796

W. Montague	Charles Holland
J. Pinkerton	E. Haskene
T. Thomas	T. Bolton
J. Pixton	T. Dunne
Walker and Orme	

John Pixton had worked as cutter on the Thames and Severn Canal a decade previously. William Montague's work on the Plow Lane to Sudbrook section had of late been "very unsatisfactory" whereas James Pinkerton was dismissed a month later and immediately sued the Canal Company for extras. On 6th January 1797, Mylne signed a new contract **(dating from the previous April)** for Stroud and Co, contractors previously for the Thames and Severn Canal, witnessed by James Dadford and John Wheeler. Pinkerton and family are described later. Thomas Dunne may have been related to William Dunn, Resident Engineer, under Jessop, of the Melton Mowbray and Oakham Canal, in 1798.

On September 26th 1796, a normal General Meeting had been held at which a resolution was passed to finish the canal as fast as possible to avoid further drain upon the finances! Mylne had attended the meeting and remained in Gloucester until October 4th, supervising the works and reporting unfavourably to the Committee on Montague's work on the section between Plow lane and Sudbrook. A few days after his departure, Dadford was engaged for a further term of four years. Routine visits followed, one upon the other, without event.

Notwithstanding impugnement Mylne had achieved something for, that very month, he and Dadford prepared:

"A Map or Plan of the Lands through which the intended line of Deviation of the Navigable Canal from Berkeley Pill to the City of Gloucester is prepared to pass in the Several Parishes of Slimbridge, Frampton, Saul, Morton Valence and Standish" showing all parcels of land, duly numbered, required for purchase. Countersigned on 30th September 1796 by the County Clerk of the Peace and witnessed by Thomas Comeline, this notice of land purchase in advance together with the resolution to complete the Canal "as fast as possible" must have reassured Mylne.

However such variations and the urgent need for permission to raise further money to cover the increased estimate, now just short of £170,000, necessitated a further Act. Between 26th December and 10th January 1797, Mylne sojourned at Gloucester, traversing the line with Dadford and "dining" with Comeline and Committee members in turn to settle the "**Bill of Variation**".

After the usual procedure the Act was passed on 1st May. Ten days later, after an absence of over four months, Mylne returned to Gloucester, to attend four Committee

Meetings, a General Meeting, a line inspection, a further survey and to "set out crossing" at Whitminster, all in the company of Dadford, his Resident Engineer. He was immediately blamed for a startling event. A draft of payment was refused by the Company's bankers and had to be met by one of the Proprietors.

Within five years an over-subscribed venture with a permitted capital of £200,000, an estimated cost of £170,000, of which less than £10,000 had been expended upon actual construction, was now virtually bankrupt. How could this be? Even allowing for lawyers' fees, salaries for the Clerk to the Company and both Chief and Resident Engineers and incidental expenses, where had the remainder gone but in dividends?

This obvious deduction failed to prevent Trye from scarifying Mylne yet again. He admitted to agreeing to Mylne's salary originally, adding sarcastically,

> "but being led to believe that every care and labour except those of simply **carrying into execution directions received** was to rest with Mr Mylne and, aware that such being the case, he must have given a great deal of personal attention to the works, and thought a deviation from the proper mode of payment might be proper, and that his terms were extremely moderate ... My opinion was altogether erroneous ... [for] but a small quantity of his personal attention has been **necessarily occupied** by the works and since our engagement[7] with Mr Dadford, scarcely any ... As for the idea ... that an Engineer may render us sufficient services by **thinking** and **contriving** for us while **sitting at his ease** in London ... [no] member is now amused by it. But while I suggest the impropriety of continuing this salary, I am far from desiring that Mr Mylne's time and services should not receive their full recompense - the labourer is undoubtedly worthy of his hire - and I am willing to give his kind of labour its highest current value. To that end I will **hypothetically** rank him with the finest artists in Navigation works - with Messrs. Whitworth and Jessop - and estimate our time accordingly."

Warming to his task, Trye now reveals his true object.

> "I postponed recommending this measure because I firmly expected that the evidence of incontrovertible facts would have produced his retirement or dismissal from the Company's service and that the new mode of payment might most conveniently begin with his successor. A small majority of shares resisting this influence and **great dissatisfaction** consequently prevailing among the Proprietors ... I suspended the execution of my purpose ... when a decision might be made with calmness and without personality ... I shall decline any personal inference in the discussion ... that I might stand free from **suspicion of motives** to which I am very superior."

In June 1797, the Committee rejected Mylne's plan for the basin, or lock as it really was, linking the main basin with the river Severn, on the grounds that its **substantiality** was too costly, but that it might be approved "if they had a national fund to draw upon."

What irony in view of the later history of the canal!

A fortnight later with no reply to the letter on the lock plan, the Committee asked Dadford for his opinion and accepted this without reference to Mylne. This happened elsewhere, putting Dadford in a difficult position, but, apparently, he so ingratiated himself with the committee that in September he was told to "report on the present state of the works and probable expenses of finishing the canal as far as the junction with the Stroud Canal" and the time considered necessary for its completion to this point. Trye's letter had been sent to Mylne who, on September 23rd, attended the Committee Meeting held, as he described it, "totally on my salary - committed it into an allowance of 4 guineas per diem." Indicative of Mylne's disinterestedness over money, he made no demur but "left to the Committee to determine upon the quantum and mode of paying" him as Engineer in the future.

He went further still; he "generously made the following proposal - that he would not in future charge the committee with any expense on the road or during his residence in the county except chaise hire." This was in character, for "he loved his profession but not the emoluments of it." By this action, Mylne might have retrieved much lost ground regarding his prestige within the Company, yet his next virtually conceded defeat, for he told the

Committee "that in consequence of some severe afflictions in his family, he had lately been prevented from attending to the concerns of this company so much as he wished to have done" and would therefore pay his own expenses for this particular trip.

He had not exaggerated his afflictions for that year his wife died, his daughter Emily died and his eldest son, Robin, had become a prisoner of war in France. These tragedies made his temperament even more volatile. Even though Farington describes him as a sociable man "much addicted to conversation and extremely exact in all his affairs", Elmes, another contemporary, had other views considering Mylne to be "a man of austere manners [and] of violent temper, [who] appeared to have a contempt for every art but his own and for every person except himself." Mylne had every reason to hold such an opinion but it hardly endeared him to the likes of Trye or Lysons or others such as Grazebrook, and Dadford too.

At the Mayor of Gloucester's "feast" on 2nd October 1797 "Dadford broke out" according to Mylne with, the following day, an "apology and pardon by Dadford". This did not prevent them both from examining the line yet again. Of particular interest in view of subsequent events, Mylne "walked to Sharpness Point"[8] with the conviction that this should be the egress to the Severn rather than Berkeley Pill. Events proved him right yet again. He left for London via Bath on 9th October.

He despatched a further report to the Committee on the destructive effect of paying out dividends with the canal as yet so far from completion. By now, however, the situation was irretrievable, as Trye now dominated it and, in December, lambasted Mylne for the excessive cost of Llantony Bridge over and above the estimate.

Worse was to follow.

The Committee wrote to Mylne proposing the omission of transom pieces and cross-planking from the invert of the double lock into the river. "Two weeks later they had had no reply from Mylne, and so they accepted Dadford's advice that the woodwork was not **really necessary** and authorised him to complete the lock according to his discretion."[9]

Mylne objected to such interference on technical design but was overruled by the Committee. There can be little doubt that "Dadford broke out" over this matter after a rebuke from Mylne that October. During the severe winter that followed a catastrophe occurred - part of the north quay wall adjacent to the lock collapsed.

"Water had entered through a hole in the bank that had been made for laying a new culvert, and the Basin had been filled almost to its intended level."[10] The bank separated the basin from the river which was in spate, so negligence caused the disaster. Mylne blamed Dadford, naturally; Dadford blamed Mylne's design.

Conway-Jones, historian of Gloucester Docks, avoids apportioning blame. Indeed he is fair to both, yet begs the question as to whose design of the wall had been built. Was it Mylne's, Jessop's or Whitworth's? Not that it matters for any unfinished wall, built at that time without backing, would have collapsed under such water pressure.

The new year, 1798, opened inauspiciously for Mylne with the receipt of a letter from the Committee, in answer to one of his, in which he had proposed remedies for making good the damage to the north wall. "In their opinion" wrote the Clerk to the Committee "nothing effectual can be done towards the reparation of the Wharf wall at this season." Mylne was urged to attend the next General Meeting in order to present his reasons and opinions as to the cause of the failure. He replied by letter deploring his inability to attend, and went on to "state what appears to me sufficiently clear - that the **present state** and failure of the said wall is and must be entirely owing to the execution of it." It was, he pointed out, exactly the same as that for the west wall (that is, Whitworth's design) but the secondary causes were those of letting the flood waters in and the delay in not completing the wall before the advent of winter. "When the Committee were [sic] pleased - rather unkind to me - to give and delegate a power to the executive Engineer **to alter the works of the lock** from my design and construction ... the Committee laid the foundation of error and I am afraid of misfortune ... Such being the confusion of duties and an improper mixture of responsibility, it is too common a trait of human nature to attend to what is the produce of its own mind most ... Alas! the apple of discord being thrown among the works, as above mentioned, what could be expected." Concluding this statement, Mylne reveals his state of mind at this time; "My domestick [sic] sensations have been of the most pungent kind by the loss of an eldest daughter after two years illness, and the having found a son in a French Prison, after an anxious search for six months ..."

Meanwhile Dadford had presented his report "on the present state of works" estimating that a connection to the Stroud Canal could be made in one year for £34,747. On receipt of Mylne's accusatory letter he declared that "Mr Mylne will not find any persons to be of his opinion for ... (the cause of failure) ... will be found to be from an ill-judged plan of building a wall on a bench of clay 9ft **from** the bottom of the bason" and that the north wall was dissimilar to the west which had been taken down through the clay wall until a gravel bottom had been reached. The 1793 plan shows this to be false.

Whatever the rights or wrongs of the case, the Committee supported Dadford. Consequently on 26th March 1798 it was resolved "that it is the opinion of this meeting that Mr Mylne no longer be employed on the business of this Company."

A curious fact now emerges. Unless away from London on other business, Mylne proved punctilious in reply to correspondence. Such was the postal service then that a fortnight's delay in receipt of an answer was certainly not unusual. Yet Mylne's Committee delegated authority to Dadford on this excuse. Mylne, however, despatched a letter and drawing of "a long section of Canal" to Wheeler, the Company Clerk on 9th April 1798, unaware that he had been dismissed. Moreover on 20th July he "wrote a long letter to Mr Wheeler on a lawsuit about Pinkerton's contract".[11]

This small anomaly points the finger at Trye's antipathy towards Mylne and the determination to be rid of him. So what happened then?

> "Work then continued under the authority of Dadford alone ... by March 1799 **the lock** was finished and the basin ready for use ... Most of the original share capital had been spent. An attempt to raise further capital had not been successful, and it was not thought proper to use the remaining money to extend the cutting of the Canal but just to finish off what had been started."[12]

A bare five and a half miles of the cut had been dug. So Dadford too was dismissed. The grandiose project had collapsed and no sane man could be prevailed upon to invest further. And why? Because out of £200,000 capital raised, only some £15,000 had been spent on actual construction - the rest frittered away by a divided, ineffectual and arrogant management.

Mylne noted in his Business Journals for 30th September 1798, "General Meeting at Gloucester." After all, he too was a shareholder. In March 1800 he entered

> "To Mr Wheeler for a sum erroneously received by Mr Jelfe and 5 years quarter interest thereof to Lady Day 1800 - to pay postage - £9-0-0."

He was nothing if not exact.

* * * * *

Two years later his exasperation at unjust treatment exploded in a letter, dated 1st February 1802, to Wheeler. Canal historians have pounced upon this with glee - Hadfield with his partiality for Jessop in particular - to dismiss Mylne as little more than an irascible old man of violent temper who, through inefficiency, brought the Gloucester and Sharpness Ship Canal to an ignominious halt. Allowing for faults on all sides, Mylne's letter cannot be ignored.

> "Well, my good Sir, I had your 2 summons to attend General Meetings on 29 Sep. and 12 Oct. ... Is there nothing going forward with the Canal? Is it to lay dormant, in a deserted state for ever? ... It always was in want of a Chancellor of the Exchequer, and a better Chairman - Till this time, I have not had leisure to reflect upon the miserable and misguided state of it and its lamentable fate. ... It is a work, that requires other talents and knowledge than a common canal cutter. From the time of Jessop's visit, I date its misfortunes. He and Dadford are mere drudges in that confined school, and both are **with't any sense of extended honour**. The G. Junction is in a dreadful state, and requires to have its difficult points all reconstructed. I have lately surveyed it. The Irish are advertising for a Resident Engineer. I think Dadford and they would fit one another to a T, for wrong heads and deficiency of knowledge."

Harsh words but true. Dadford can be dismissed kindly as inexperienced for he is never heard of again. Jessop and his relationship with Mylne is examined later.

Meanwhile the brave project had foundered; the basin lay empty and disused; the five mile cut silted up as a stretch of stagnant water. And still the shareholders met several times a year. What they thought of Trye and Lysons is unrecorded. In 1806 hopes were raised by a project for a tramroad from the basin to Cheltenham involving trans-shipment of coal from Severn Trows berthing in the basin. Trye made sure of a branch of the tramroad to his stone quarries at Leckhampton Hill.[13] Because of this, the project took five years to materialise but opened finally, in midsummer 1811, by which time Trye, Lysons and Mylne were all dead.[14]

Previous to this, however, Mylne had reason to visit Gloucester and, on 1st August 1809, noted that he had "viewed by myself the present old bridge (Llantony) and canal works etc. - all night at Gloucester - wrote letters to both attorneys (Welles and Comeline)." A year later on 10th November 1810 "[He] awaited upon Mr Disney relating to a survey of part of the Gloucester and Berkeley Canal."[15]

Volatile Mylne might have been but many still valued his expertise. Trye and Lysons might have served Gloucester better had they followed suit for, between them, they effectively denied success.

As Thomas Telford declared two years later

"In Britain ... useful works have been constructed at the expense, and under the direction of particular, and frequently very limited districts, communities, or individuals, whose chief object has been, in general, money."

He had no realisation then that he, himself, would be the instrument of the completion of the Gloucester and Sharpness Canal in 1827.

NOTES

1. Unless noted otherwise excerpts quoted are from Gloucester and Berkeley Company records 1793-1809.
2. Mylne's Journals.
3. This plan, signed by Mylne and Dadford, in the House of Lords' Library shows deviations of the line, later adopted, to shorten it, together with all properties affected.
4. Gloucester Docks. H. Conway-Jones 1984. Alan Sutton Publishing Ltd. County Library Series. It is possible that Blackburn was an ally of Trye, for this statement is almost too convenient at this particular time. There is no mention of Blackburn in Mylne's Business Journal. No records so far reveal his identity, occupation or wealth.
5. Locks and water levels on the Gloucester and Berkeley Canal. A. Richardson. Canal and Railway Historical Society, 1987.
6. This one statement destroys his case, confirming as it does the payment of dividends before completion of the work.
7. "Directions received" prove the point of conflict; "Since our engagement with Mr Dadford" equally so, indicating Dadford's inabilities and the expectation that a Chief Engineer should make up the deficiencies of the Resident Engineer - the situation was clearly impossible.
8. Ibid. 2.
9. Ibid. 4.
10. Ibid. 4.
11. Ibid. 2.
12. Ibid. 4.
13. Ibid. 4.
14. Mylne actually died in December that year.
15. Ibid. 2.

5

DORMANCY

"My profession is as perfectly personal as that of a physician."
(John Smeaton.)

So the great venture had foundered. By 1800 the works lay idle and neglected; not even the Dock was put to use. Wheeler remained as Clerk to the Canal Company which still held regular meetings to discuss various methods of reviving the venture. "When difficulties arose" Hadfield stated "it was the custom of the Committee to call in other engineers to make a report - The Gloucester and Berkeley, engineered by Mylne, was reported on at various times by Jessop, Whitworth, Telford, Hodgkinson and Rennie." Whilst factually correct, the inference is less so.

Clearly Mylne never "designed" the line and the reports of Jessop and Whitworth have been considered. The other four were involved after Mylne's dismissal and death: the period now under examination. From Wheeler's successor as Clerk in 1813/14, John Upton, can be gleaned information contained, but ignored hitherto, in his "Observations" to "The Proprietors and Subscribers" in 1815.

Why he accepted the post is unknown, but when appointed he made a study of company records. In doing so he became imbued with the theory of engineering to such an extent - it changed his life - as to be instrumental in resuscitating the venture. Within the flowery verbiage, common then, of his treatise are obvious hints of what had really happened to cause the cessation of work and what then followed.

[In his introduction, Upton wished to shed] "light upon subjects ... too long neglected and obscured from various causes [and to] convey information ... only obtained by a tedious search into the former proceedings." [Cautious in his approach to avoid offence - he was, after all, a servant of the Company - he continued:] "My ideas ... differ materially from certain **received opinions** - and **favourite theories** - adopted from **mistaken** principles ... perhaps [now] overturned." [It cannot escape notice that this was aimed at Trye and Lysons, by then both dead.]

"From the records," [the treatise opens] "two persons" [were employed] "to survey and **lay down** the line ... and terminations." [One line] "drawn by a Mr Clowes, an engineer - was to go on low land, (according to Mr Mylne's report, for the plan is not in the Canal Office.)[1] and terminates just below, or on the south side of Sharpness Point."

"[The other plan] by a Mr Hall, a land-surveyor[2] [was more inland] through deeper cutting ... which Mr Mylne observes 'will be much more expensive ... and to terminate at Berkeley Pill [both were practicable] and might be adopted which the Committee judged fittest. [Neither plan provided for] many basons or harbours for shipping."

Upton declared forcibly in favour of the "Clowes" plan and then quotes a letter from Mylne to the Committee on "the subject of a proper entrance" from the Severn.

'The termination and entrance at Berkeley Pill never was a favourite with me, it was **resolved** on before I was concerned ... [and] all that I attempted was to render it feasible and intelligible."

[Upton then makes a revealing statement.]

"By this it would appear, that when he was first sent for, the entrance at Berkeley Pill was considered as a sort of **sine qua non** in the business; and if so Mr Mylne was not censurable for projecting that entrance."

[And here comes the crunch.]

"If he was thought the most capable of the three [Clowes and Hall being the others] (as is apparent from his having been selected to direct the works) it seems strange that he was not desired to point out the best line and the most fit terminations which **he could find**, for surely none will deny that this is one of the most important duties of the profession, and much better understood by practical than theoretical men; and neither Mr Hall, the land-surveyor, nor the Committee, could be expected to know anything relative to the execution of such works, or even what sort of entrance could be made. The conclusions can only be safely drawn by those who have a **practical** knowledge of such matters: but when an engineer has no latitude allowed him - no power of deviating from **fixed** opinions - nothing but a servile obedience to the instructions and **previous determinations** of those who employ him - it is not much unlike a patient **dictating** to his physician, who of all men should be the first consulted, and a carte blanche presented to him."

[Upton, bit between the teeth, gallops on.]

"Soon after the works commenced, a part of the erroneous line ... so **blindly adopted**, was in a slight degree improved by a second application to Parliament ... but this did not amount to even half a measure; and left the undertaking encumbered with nearly the same difficulties as before."[3]

[Upton reckoned that Mylne's "improved estimate" was **correct** but] "after proceeding with the works some time, it was found that several articles had cost the Company much more money than had been **specified** they should do ... so Mr Mylne was discontinued and the person [acting] under him (or, at least, was supposed to do so) was preferred [i.e. James Dadford]."

[Upton then criticised harshly the work carried out under Dadford as] "very injudiciously done. And I am aware," [he continues] "that in all large undertakings **abuses** will ... occur; but of this Canal [from information received] several years before I saw it ... my opinion [is] of the great negligence of **some persons** engaged.

The Committee acted rather incautiously, when, in removing Mr Mylne[4], they preferred Mr Dadford, who of all men, was the most unfit: for he served an apprenticeship to a different business, and had no experience in such work, or even common masonry or carpentry; and, in either his natural or acquired abilities, was as much inferior to Mr Mylne as a glow-worm is to the sun."

Robert Mylne had one advocate, postmortem then. Upton never met nor knew Mylne but on the basis of Company Minutes, letters and drawings, became his champion and set the record straight.

Upton continues his retrospect of events culled from Company records, before his own appointment.

"Things remained in a ... torpid state for some time: when one of the Proprietors, despairing of ever being able to continue the Canal to Berkeley Pill for want of the necessary resources, thought of forming a nearer junction with the Severn at a place at Hock Crib,"[5] [also called Hock Cliff.]

In spite of adverse comments from local trowmen and pilots "Still this gentleman resolved not to lose sight of his object ... and **determined to persevere** especially as three men were found who countenanced the idea." Ralph Walker, the engineer of East India Docks in London, was asked to report but proved a disappointment in making clear he favoured Berkeley Pill. Walker's advice was dismissed and a Bill put to Parliament for a terminus at Hock Crib.

A subscription was opened but failed to reach the required target. The Committee then "applied to Mr Jessop and Mr John Hodgkinson (well known as a railway engineer) for an estimate of the expense of making the Canal ... to Hock Crib."

At this point one senses Upton's censure of Jessop in stating:

"Mr Jessop attended the committee, in consequence, with an estimate **signed** by Mr J. Hodgkinson amounting to £81,300 but which ... did **not** include the purchase of the land, damages, wide places for vessels to pass, supply of water for feeding the Canal and several other matters."

Not content with this, our "unknown" proprietor insisted upon a further opinion. According to Hadfield "the ardour of enterprise of the Proprietors of the Gloucester and

Berkeley Canal carried them to success through great difficulties." This is being "economical with the truth" indeed. The wretched Committee now applied to John Rennie who was considerably more unpopular with his colleagues than ever was Mylne. Rennie went over the top in recommending, in addition to an inner harbour at Hock Crib, a tide harbour and a pier for protection "of vessels using the Canal" estimated at £128,656 but "if funds were low, the pier in question might be deferred."

> [Upton commented with irony] "that without such a pier, vessels coming **too late** upon a tide to **enter** the locks, would have **no where to run, and therefore would be liable to be swamped!!!**"

Rennie's report finally silenced the "unknown" proprietor who, when a tramroad was proposed in 1806 from Gloucester, passing by the Docks, to Cheltenham to join the railway there, insisted upon a branch to the stone quarries at Leckhampton which he happened to own. The tramroad opened in 1811.

> "The Canal Company strongly supported the project but at first did nothing about opening the basin."

Indeed, it "erected gates across the rails" to collect a toll. But in 1812 "the Canal Company reversed their [sic] earlier policy and decided to open the basin."[6] This caused Upton problems of water supply to the basin due to lock leakage and lack of feeders. He overcame this by the installation of a pump engine, lifting water from the Severn to the dock.

By now Upton had assumed the title of Resident Engineer and Clerk and, as such, circulated his treatise to his employers. To make the basin acceptable for vessels to berth and trans-ship goods he had to dredge accumulated silt from both lock and basin.

> "and here it is but doing justice to the memory of the late Mr Mylne to observe that he mentioned this subject in one of his letters: 'I was very sorry to see some neglect in the state of the gates when in a late journey through Gloucester'."

This must have been in 1810.

Upton then made the point that, after Mylne had been dismissed, it was Dadford who supervised the cutting of the line to Hardwicke at a cost of £100,000. Mylne's figure on dismissal had been a mere £7,000. This accounts for Upton's condemnation of the work done - bank slips, towing paths and bridge masonry being "shamefully done, most of the piers being **split**: and when the money paid is contrasted with the different articles executed, and the price of materials and labour is kept in view, there appears a **striking disproportion**." Harsh words indeed, to which he added "[These] serve to confirm my opinion of the great negligence of some persons engaged." For negligence, read corruption.

In Upton, Mylne had a good friend. Upton had no axe to grind, for when he submitted his "Observations" in 1815, the participants in the debacle of the first stage of this "Unprofitable Pie" had died - Trye, Lysons, Mylne, Jessop and Whitworth.

Upton, now a "Marine Engineer", dismissed the line to Hock Crib with scorn. "I will challenge any respectable engineer to say one word in favour of Hock Crib" as the river terminus, due to the shoals and the expense of a pier. He also pointed out the total lack of water feeders along the line. Turning to Berkeley Pill he accepted this to be a reasonable terminus but not the line to it.

> "It is certain, that the original line laid down by [those] who first surveyed it [i.e. Hall and Pinnell] has involved the scheme in considerable error and disgrace ... that would occasion enormous expenses" [due to unnecessary cutting and faulty levels.] [Upton then claimed (pace Clowes and Mylne)] "a good and extremely favourable line has been found and may be adopted; if **party and prejudice** are not suffered to overwhelm the interests of Subscribers; for it is truly deplorable to observe that **obstinacy, self-interest and prejudice** have formed a powerful coalition to render the completion of the Noble Canal obnoxious in the public estimation."

Some pages on, he revealed Sharpness Point as his proposed terminus, more practical by far than Berkeley Pill, spelling out in detail the advantages, including cheaper land purchase of the altered line. Backing his contention with a plan and various estimates, he made out a sound case formulated by intense study and even nodded to the spirit of his admired mentor. "Let the entrance [at Sharpness] be where it may. I would advise a double set of locks, to save water; one for trows and small craft, and the other for larger vessels, **as Mr Mylne intended.**"

By his exertions, Upton vindicated both Clowes, responsible for the initial concept, and Mylne who unwisely allowed himself to be entrapped by an impossible situation. Alas, Upton himself fell victim before long. Meanwhile his recommendation was well received and adopted by the Canal Committee: the next task being to raise finance. This proved the rub, but help was at hand.

The demobilisation of armed forces at the end of the Napoleonic War in 1815 caused severe unemployment which the government attempted to obviate by setting up the Exchequer Bill Loan Commission Board, two years later. Authorised to make substantial loans on projects offering work to unskilled labour, the Board appointed Thomas Telford as technical advisor on Civil Engineering schemes, to assess the merit of applications for loans submitted.

The Gloucester and Berkeley Canal Company made an early application for a loan to complete the Canal in accordance with John Upton's plan. Telford was despatched to prepare a report on viability. Wasting no time, he delivered this, with an estimate of £125,723 for completion, adding that "anything short of this would be a delusion and a disgrace."[7]

The Canal Company had some hope at last of realising its tarnished dream.

NOTES

1. This suggests that it had been deliberately destroyed.
2. 1792, drawn by Thomas Pinnell, Hall's partner.
3. 1795 Act.
4. Historians have ignored Upton's report hitherto, yet only he knew what had caused Mylne's dismissal.
5. Surely this must have been Trye. If not, then Rev. D. Lysons, Topographer, whose uncle, Dr D. Lysons, had died in 1800.
6. Gloucester Docks. H. Conway-Jones. Alan Sutton and Gloucester County Library. 1988.
7. Thomas Telford and the Gloucester and Berkeley Canal. G. Neville Crawford. Industrial Archaeology Review XI.2 Spring 1989. Copy supplied by the Ironbridge Gorge Museum Trust.

Illustrations.

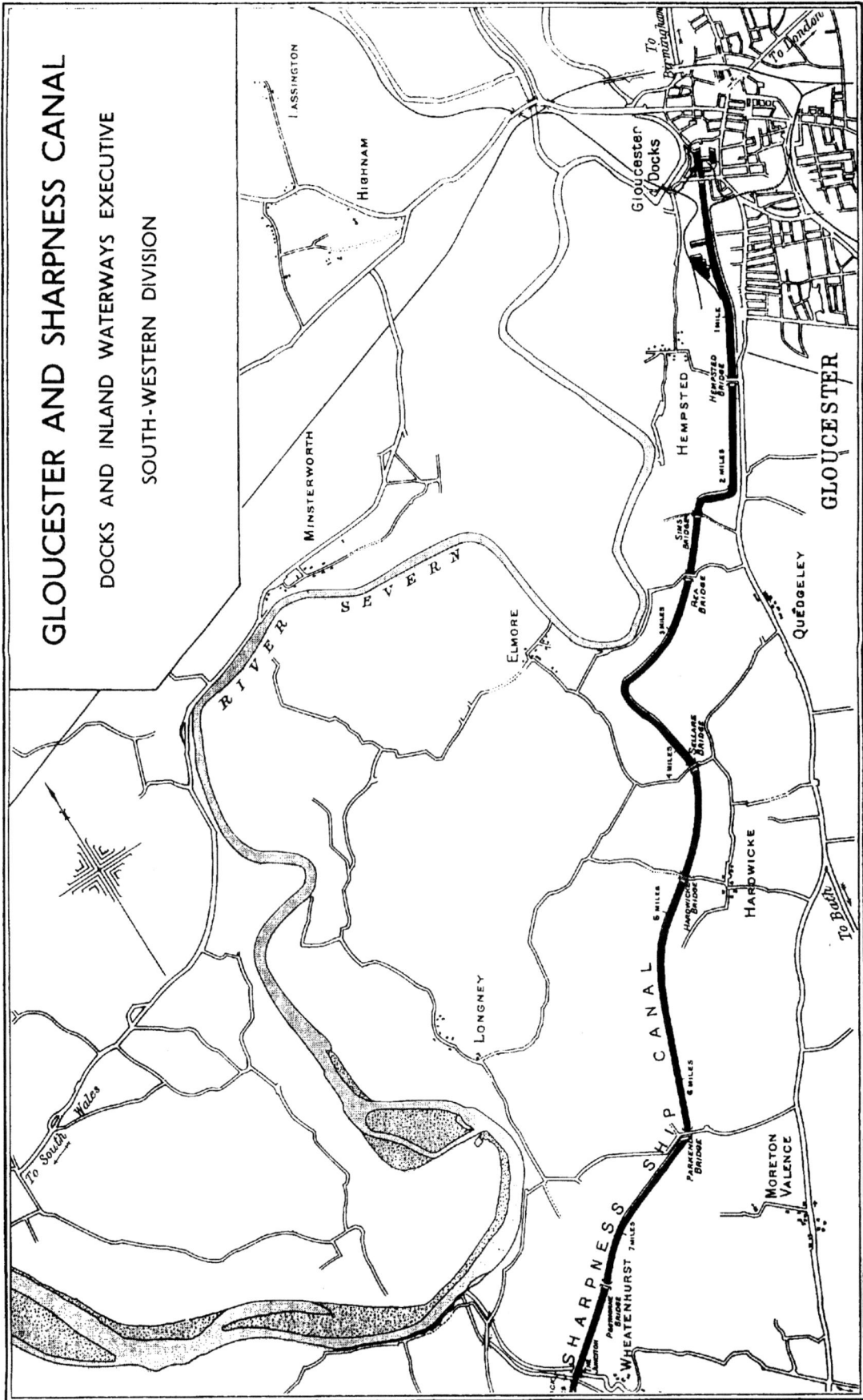

GLOUCESTER AND SHARPNESS CANAL

DOCKS AND INLAND WATERWAYS EXECUTIVE

SOUTH-WESTERN DIVISION

Plate 1

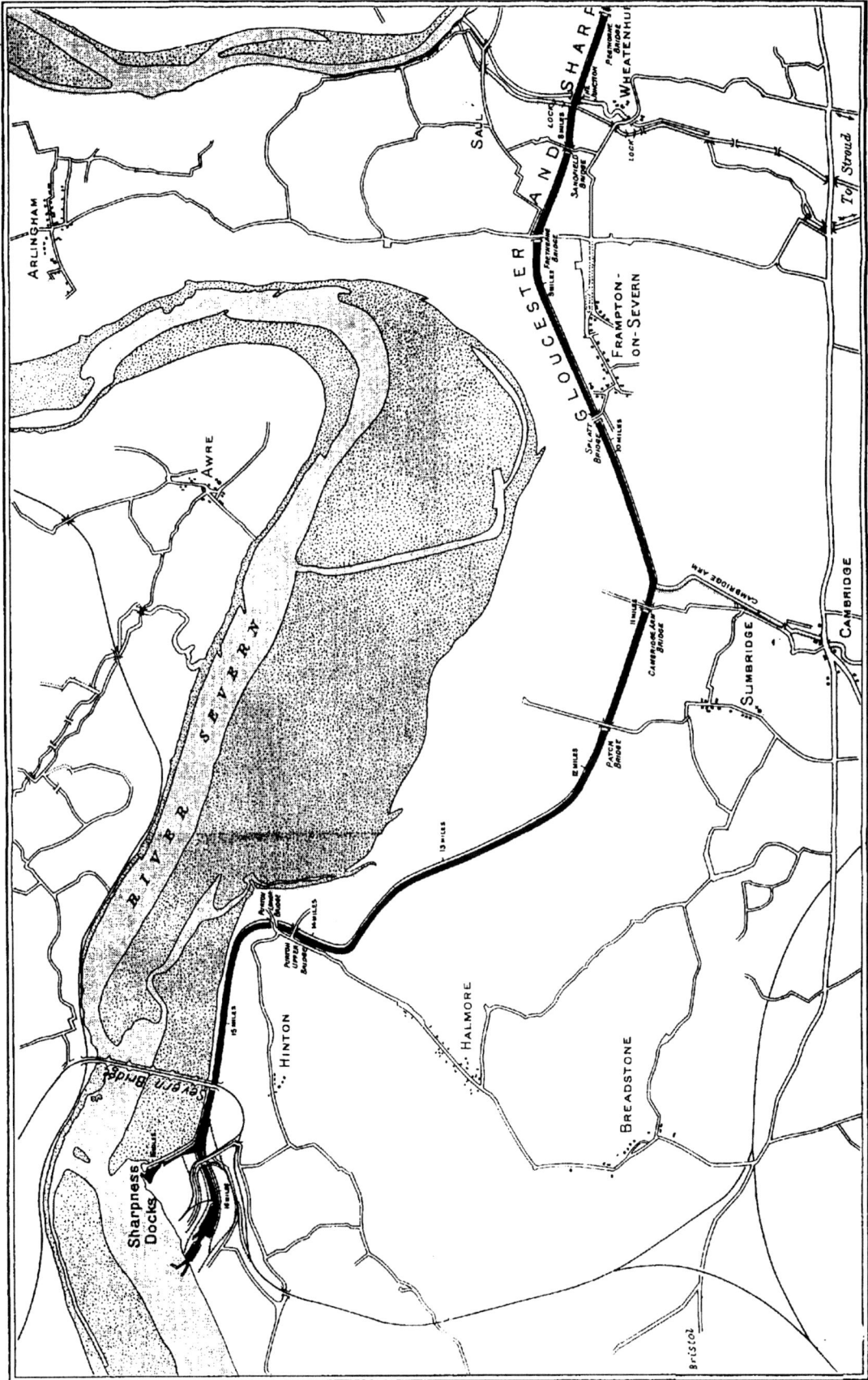

Plate 2

Plate 3

b

Plate 4

a

a

b

Plate 5

EDIFICES of LONDON. — BRIDGES.

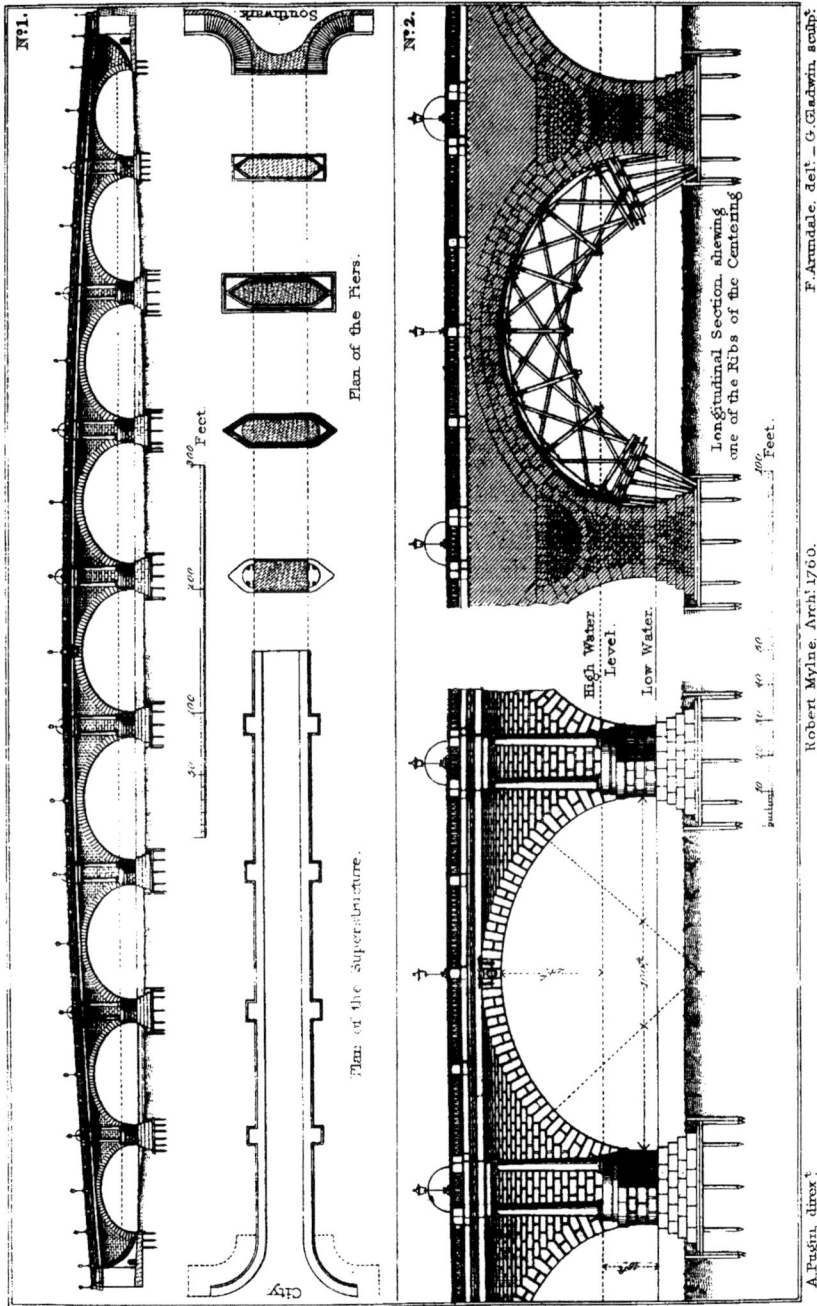

N.º1.

Southwark

Plan of the Piers.

3.⁰⁰ 1.⁰⁰ 2.⁰⁰ 3.⁰⁰ Feet

Plan of the Superstructure.

City

N.º2.

Longitudinal Section, shewing
one of the Ribs of the Centering

100 Feet

High Water
Level.

Low Water.

10 20 30 40 50 100 Feet

A. Pugin, direx.ᵗ

Robert Mylne. Arch.ᵗ 1760.

F. Arundale. del.ᵗ — G. Gladwin sculp.ᵗ

BLACKFRIARS BRIDGE.

N.º1. West Elevation and Plan.— 2. Elevation and Section of Centre Arch.

London, Published Jan.ᵞ 1828 by J. Taylor, High Holborn.

Plate 6

a

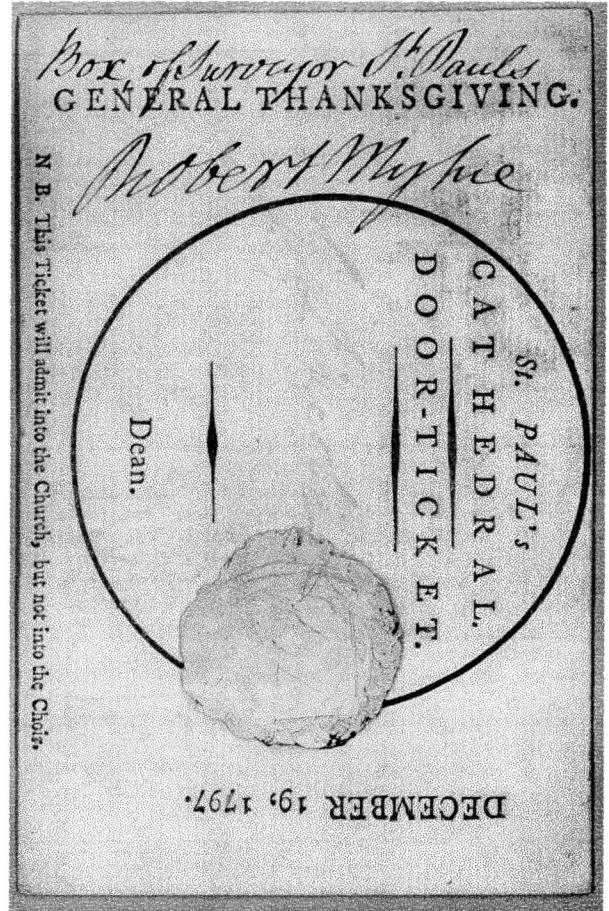

b

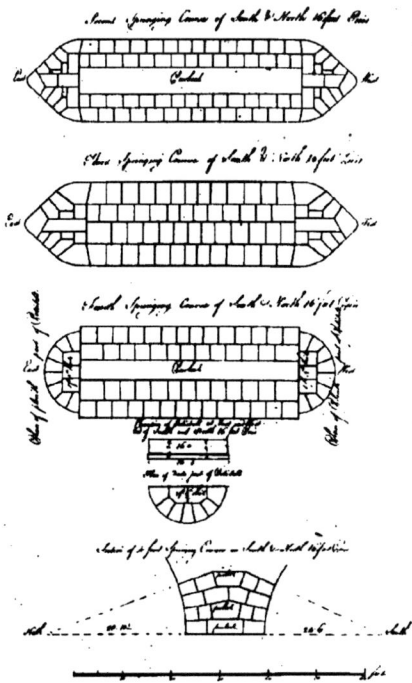

c

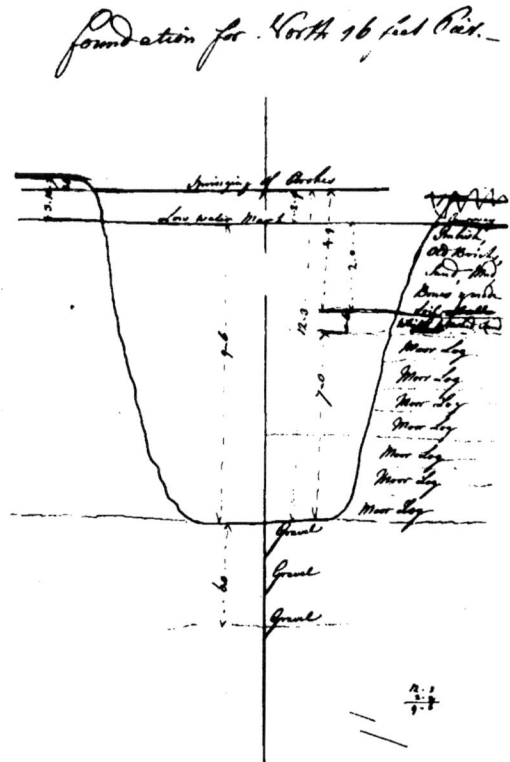

d

Plate 7

b

a

Plate 8

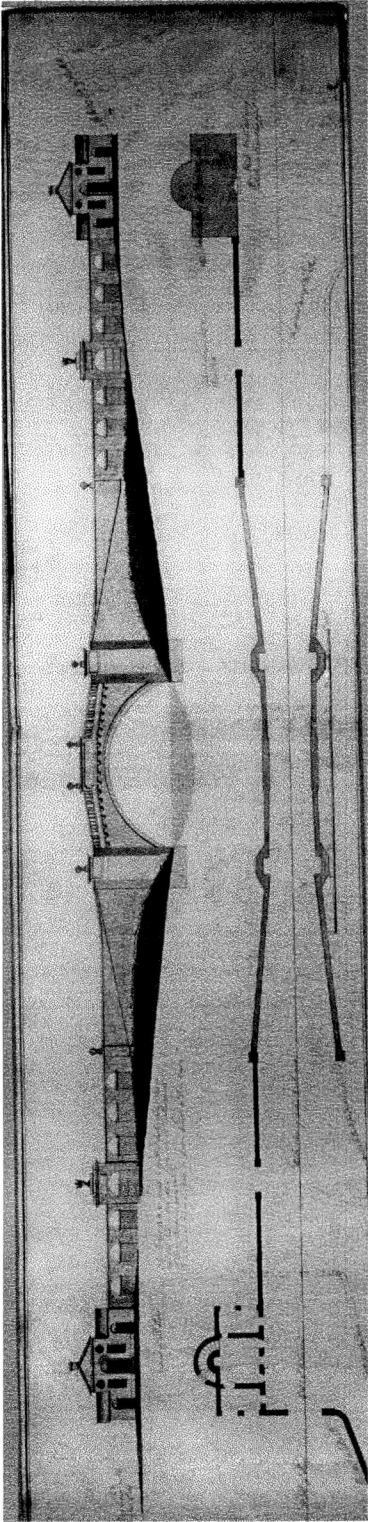

a

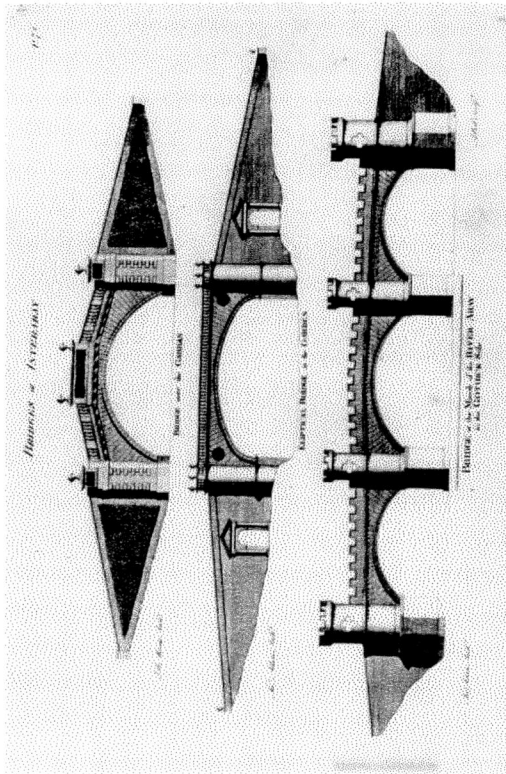

b

Plate 9

a

b

Plate 10

Plate 11

Plate 12

Plate 13

Plate 14

a

b

Plate 15

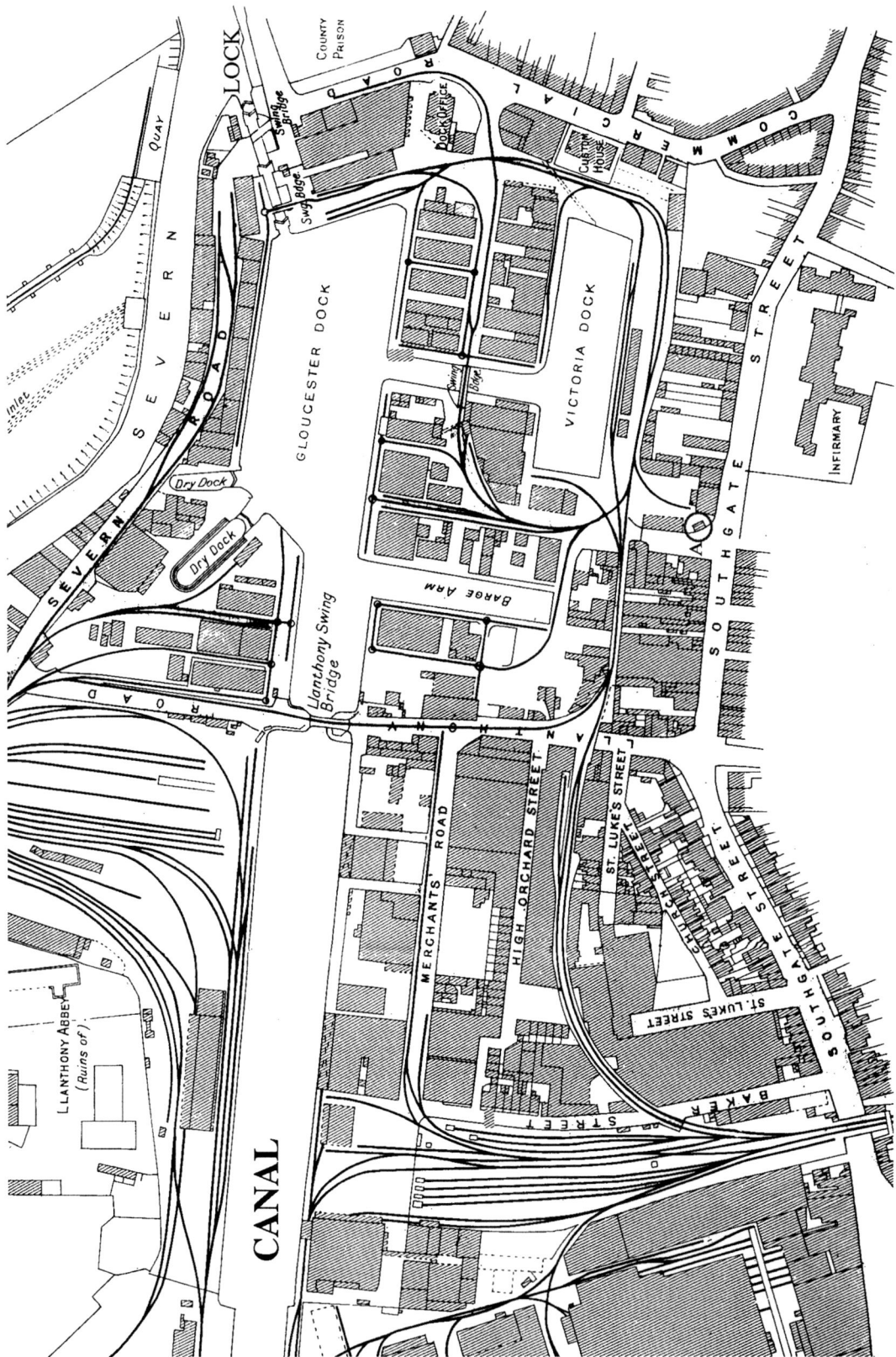

Plate 16

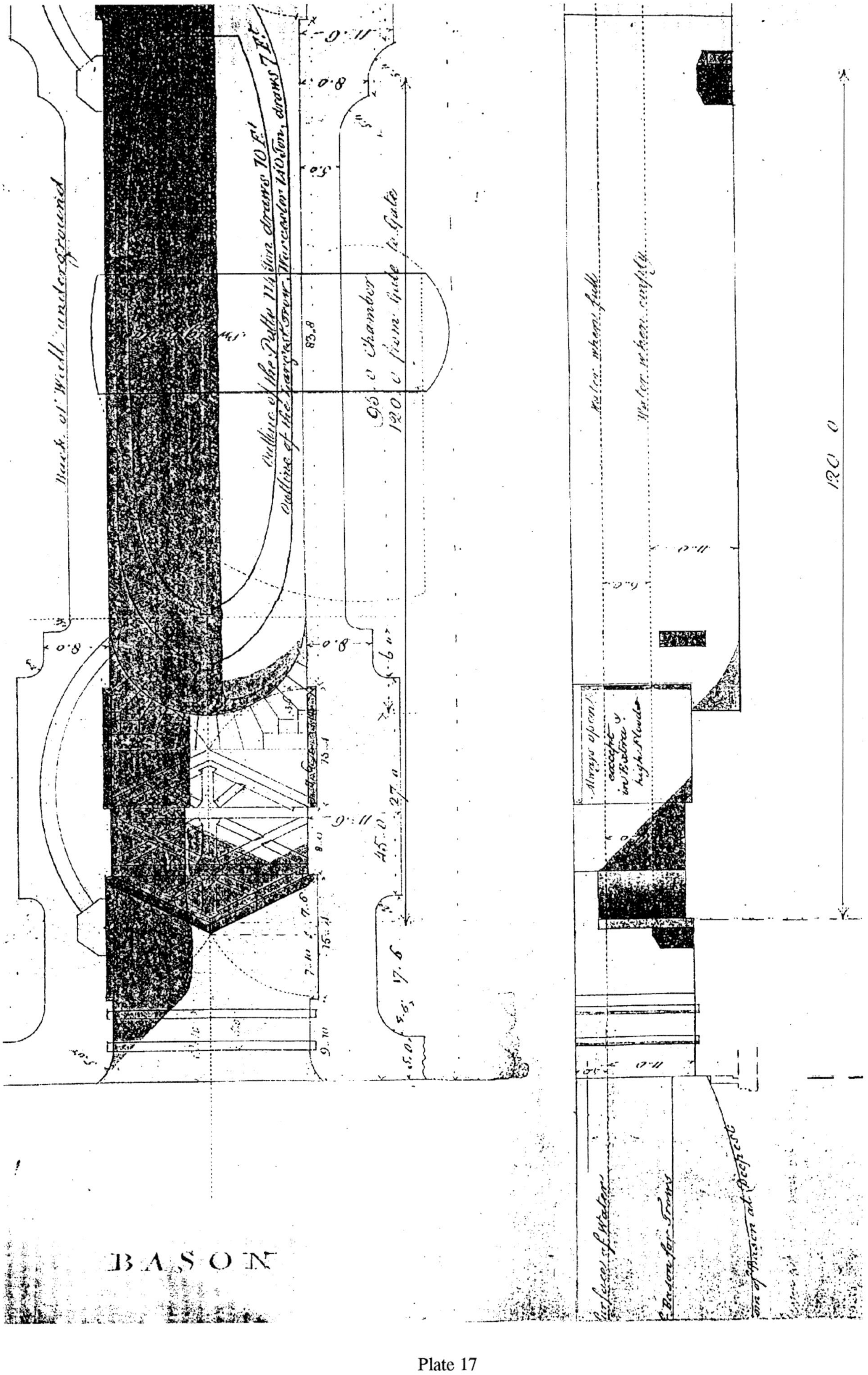

BASON

Back of Wall underground

Outline of the Petto Walter draws 10 Et

Outline of the largest Frem Worcester 150 Ton, draws 7 Et

95 ft Chamber

120 ft from side to Gate

83.8

Water when full

Water when empty

Always open except in extra high Flood

120 0

first level of Water

Bottom of Frem

of Apron at present

Plate 17

level of the Quay

Water level — Top of Gates — Water level

Wharf

18.0

UPPER N^{rn} CILL

Floor of Entrance
Depth all round Basin
Depth of the footings
Depth of middle part

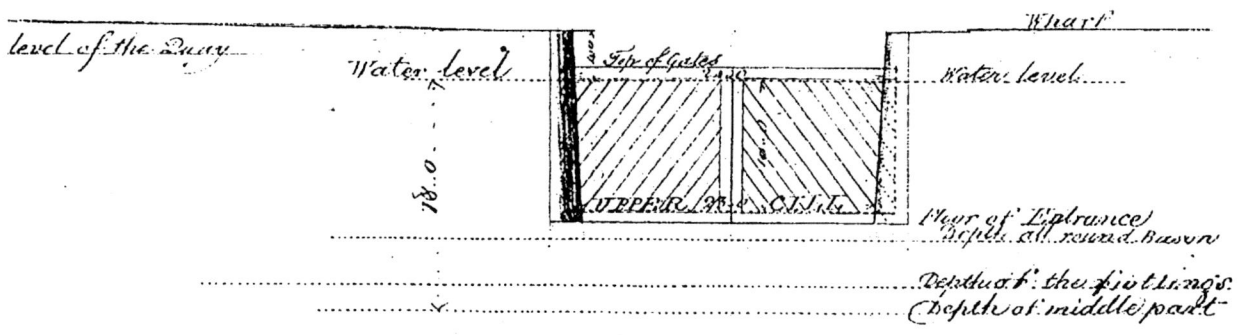

Section, at the
Entrance to the Lock

a

Water of Canal — Surface of Quay

Top of Gates

Water in Lock when Empty

Water in Lock lower'd & emptd
Water partly Kept back
Water lowest in River

Lowest in the River

Bottom of Lock

Bottom of River

Surface of Cill, & bottom of River, opp^d Custom house

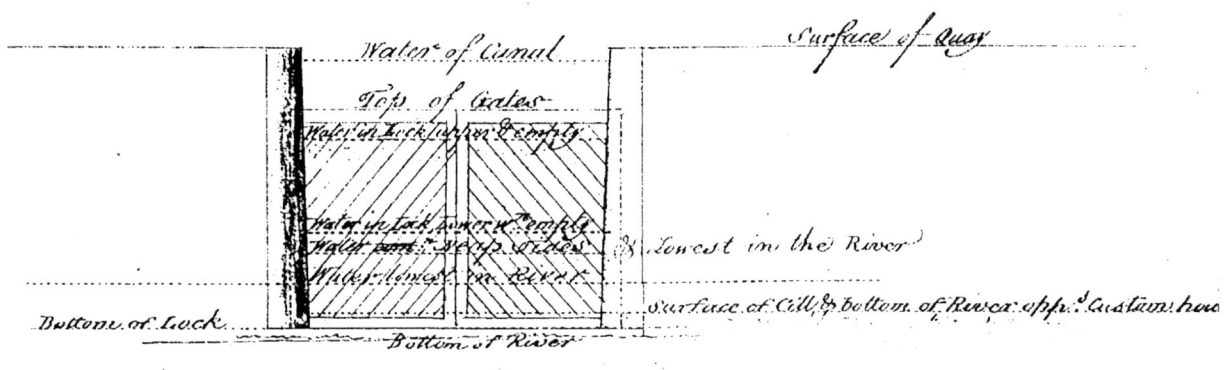

Section of the
Entrance to the Lock
next the Severn

b

Plate 18

Plate 19

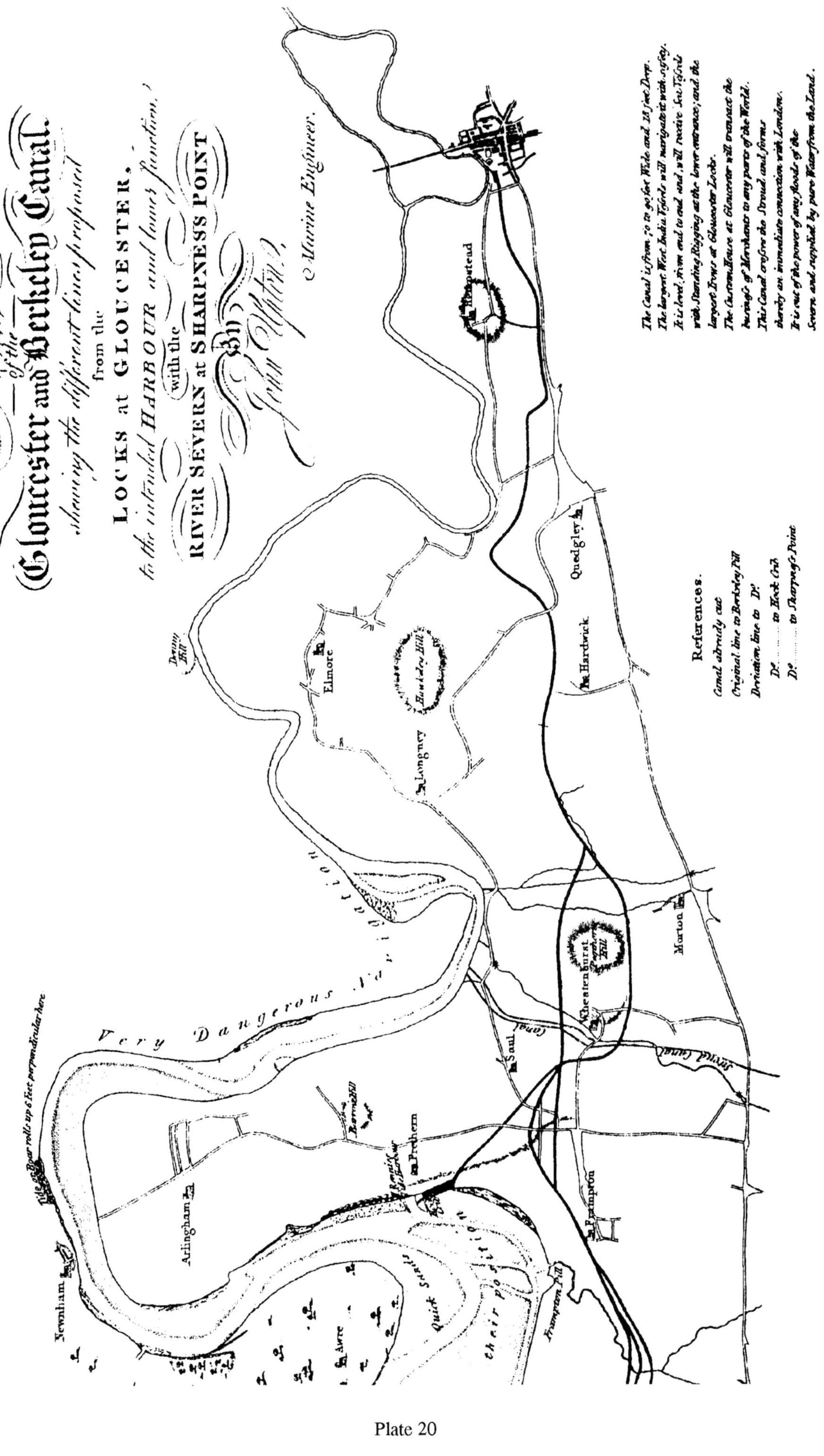

Plan of the Gloucester and Berkeley Canal.

shewing the different lines proposed

from the

LOCKS at GLOUCESTER,

to the intended HARBOUR and lower junction,

with the

RIVER SEVERN at SHARPNESS POINT

John Upton.

Marine Engineer.

References.

Canal already cut

Original line to Berkeley Pill

Deviation line to D°

D°   to Hock Crib

D°   to Sharpness Point

The Canal is from 70 to 90 feet Wide and 18 feet Deep.
The largest West India Vessels will navigate it with safety.
It is level, stem and to end, and will receive Sea Vessels
with Standing Rigging at the lower entrance, and the
largest Barges at Gloucester Locks.
The Accumulation at Gloucester will warrant the
buying of Merchants to any parts of the World.
This Canal crosses the Stroud and forms
thereby an immediate connection with London.
It is out of the power of any floods of the
Severn and is supplied by pure Water from the Land.

Very Dangerous Navigation

Newnham

Arlingham

Barrow Hill

Prthern

Fretherne

Saul (Out)

Framilode (Out)

Frampton

Chestenhurst Hill

Morton

Wh. Hardwick

Quedgley

Longney

Elmore

Barkeley Hill

Denny Hill

Westend

Plate 20

b

a

Plate 21

a

b

Plate 22

b

a

Plate 23

a Sharpness. Old Docks, shewing Severn Bridge.

b

Plate 24

a

b

Plate 25

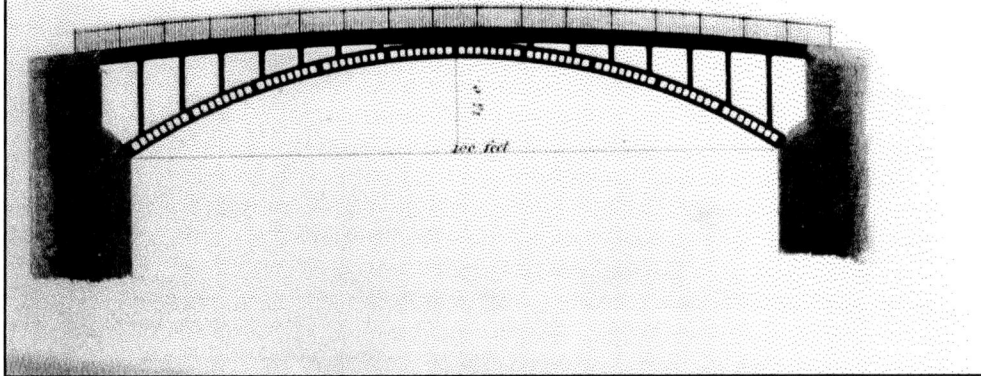

BRIDGE.   PLATE XCIV.

Bristol Bridge.

100 feet

a

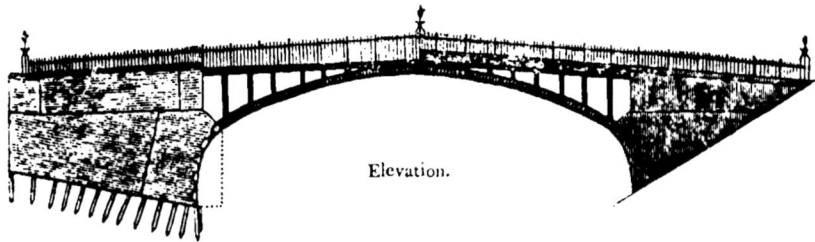

Elevation.

b

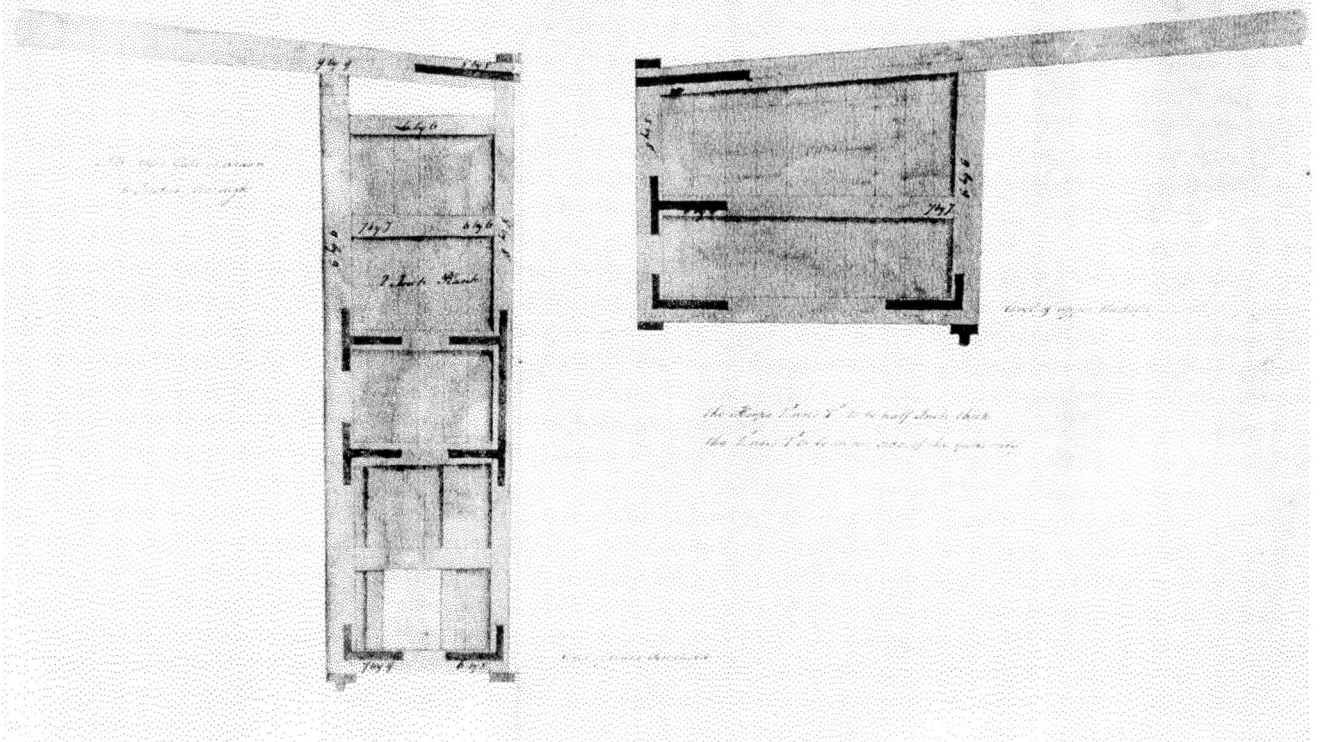

GATES of the narrow Locks for the Ellesmere Canal
(for Locks of 9 feet wide)

c

Plate 26

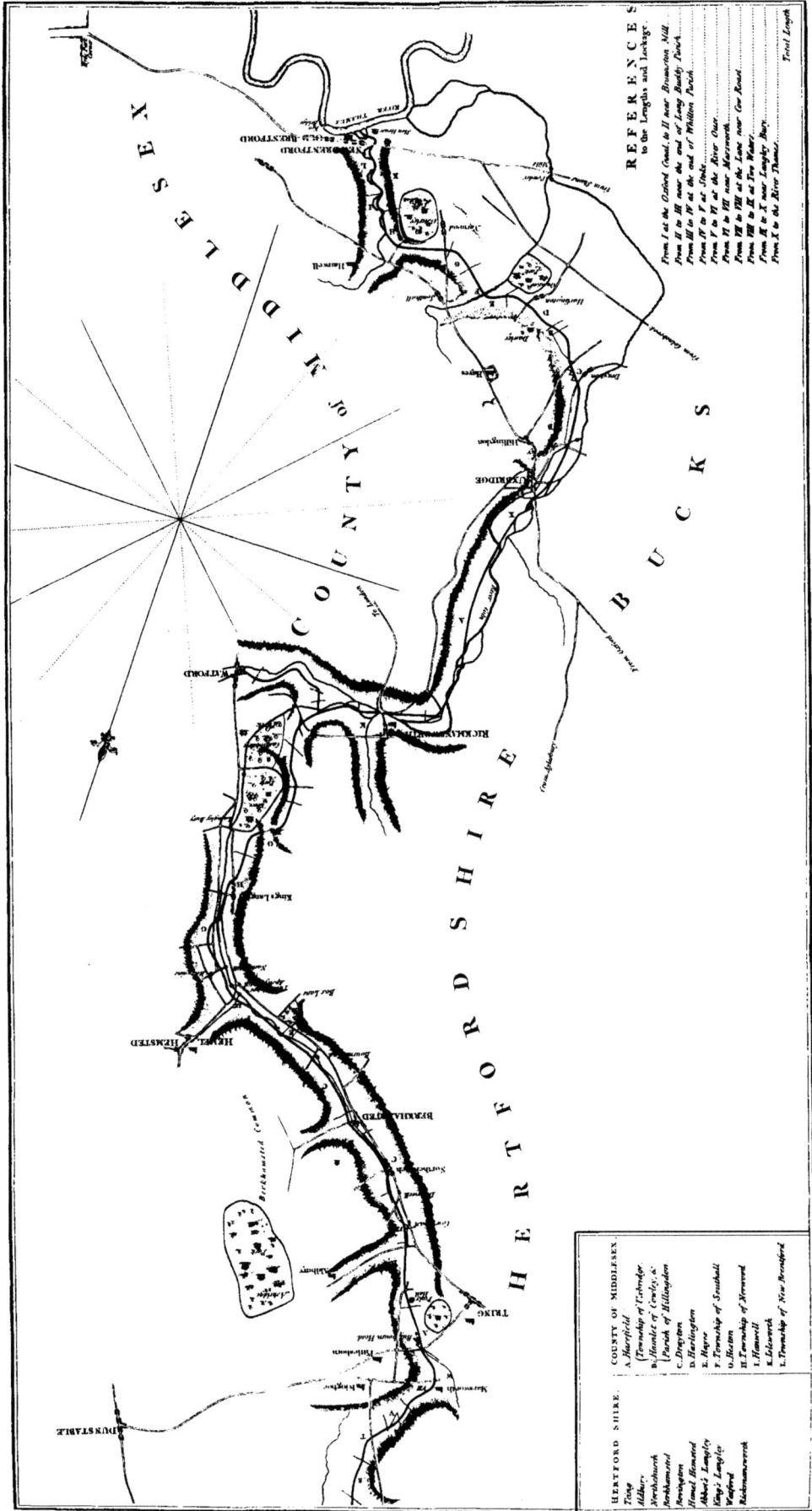

Plate 27

a

b

Plate 28

Plate 29

a

b

Plate 30

A PLAN of the
RIVER THAMES
from the KENNETs MOUTH to
LONDON,
Shewing the
INTENDED CANAL
from
SUNNING LOCK to MONKEY ISLAND
and from thence
(BY ORDER OF THE CITY OF LONDON)
Surveyed to Isleworth
By Mr Brindley.

Engraved by Thomas Jefferys Geographer to the King, 1770.

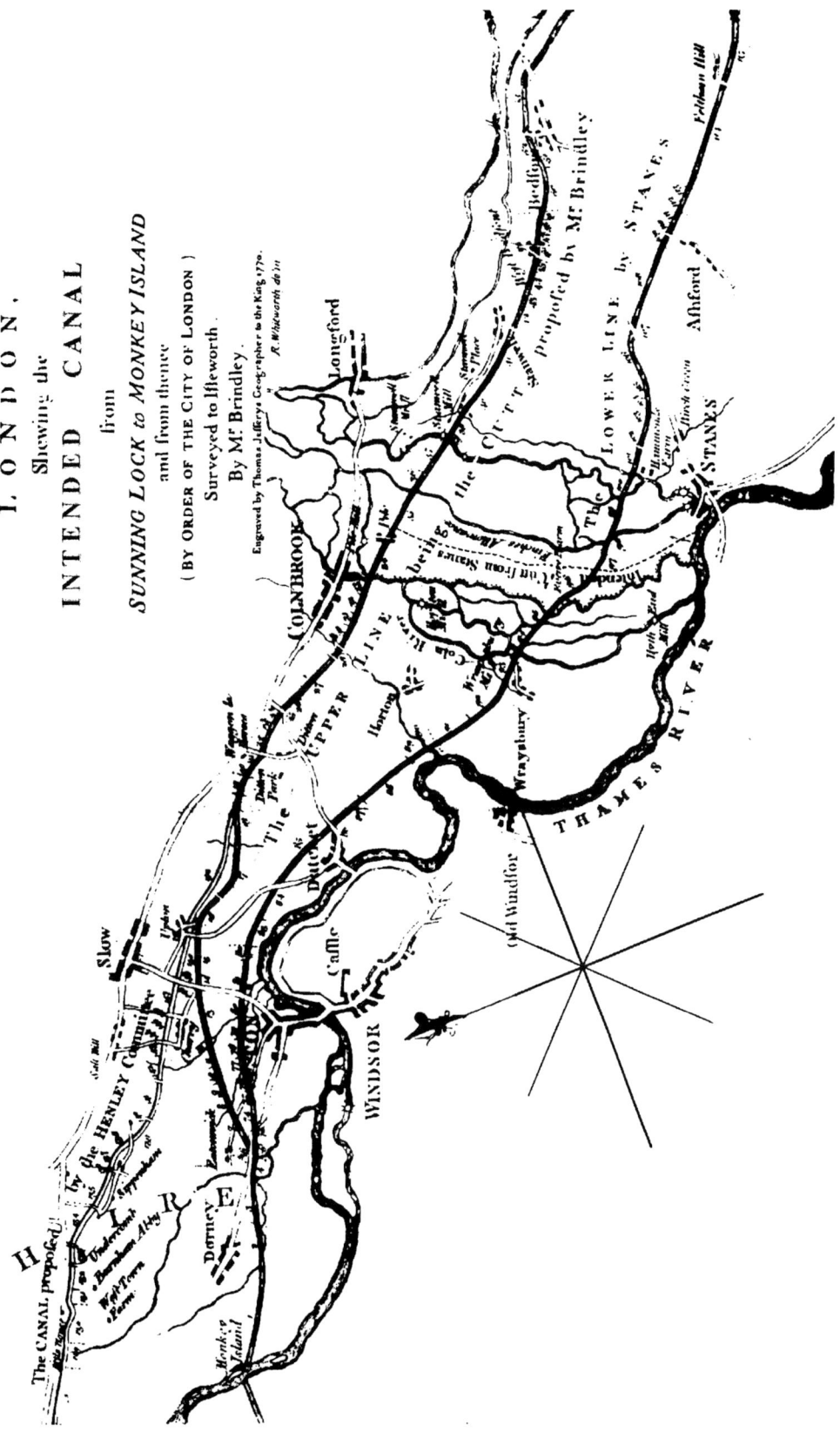

R. Whitworth de'in

BERKSHIRE

The CANAL proposed by the HENLEY Committee

Monkey Island

Dorney

West Town

Boveney

Boveham Abby

Under Lock

Appearance

Salt Mill

Slow

WINDSOR

Castle

The Disgost

Hampton

Upper

Winter Bourn

UPPER LINE

COLNBROOK

Colne River

The Bett

North End Mill

Wraysbury

Old Windsor

THAMES RIVER

STANES

Canal from Stanes to Isleworth intended

The LOWER LINE by STANES

Longford

the CITY LINE proposed by Mr Brindley

Ashford

Feltham Hill

Plate 31

a

b

Plate 32

Robert Mylne.

Plate 33

6

PONTIFEX MAXIMUS

"I admire commercial enterprise ... but I hold that the aim and end of all ought not to be a mere bag of money, but something far higher and far better."

(Thomas Telford.)

Thomas Telford (1757-1834) has never lacked sycophants. "An engineer of stature at least as great as any before or since - well-called 'the colossus of roads' and 'Pontifex maximus'."[1] or, as Burton more aptly states, the man "who apart from his canal work, closed the gap between the canal age of the eighteenth century and the age of nineteenth century engineering achievement."[2]

A lowlander Scot, Telford began his working life as a "journeyman mason".[3] He moved south in 1782 with ambition to become an architect, to which end he cultivated patrons one of whom, William Pulteney of Bath, obtained his appointment as County Surveyor of Shropshire in 1786.

Such were the demands of the Canal Mania in 1793, he was appointed that year 'General Agent, Surveyor, Engineer, Architect and Overlooker of the Works' by the Ellesmere Canal Company to the Chief Engineer, William Jessop. At least Telford had more experience of construction work than Dadford, and soon revealed a flair more for engineering than architecture. So much so that when Josiah Clowes, Chief Engineer of the Shrewsbury Canal (after the debacle of the Hereford and Gloucester) died in 1795, Telford took over.

Amongst the proprietors of this were William and John Reynolds and John Wilkinson, all ironmakers connected with the Quaker Darby family business of Coalbrookdale who, when Telford's first task was to rebuild the recently destroyed masonry aqueduct over the river Tern at Longden[4], proposed a replacement in cast iron.

"Telford took enthusiastically to the idea and went to work with William Reynolds on designing the structure."[5]

This, of course, was twenty years after the famous Ironbridge had been built in 1779 over the Severn at Coalbrookdale, by Abraham Darby III to a design by Thomas F. Pritchard of Shrewsbury, renowned as the first of its kind in the world. Pritchard, however, had made in 1775, a "Design of a Bridge constructed on a Cast Iron Centre" the rest being of masonry.

The year previously Robert Mylne sent John, 5th Duke of Argyll, a drawing of the "Castle or metal bridge Cost £2,500" at Inverary. Never built, it is "probably the earliest surviving design of an iron bridge". Moreover it was "in the Chinese fashion", equally innovative then.[6]

The third "projector of iron bridges in Britain was neither a bridge-builder nor an ironfounder but a political writer." Tom Paine, author of 'The Rights of Man' in 1787, brought from America to London a model of a cast iron bridge of 400ft span to show Sir Joseph Banks, the president of the Royal Society, and a member of The Smeatonian Society. On advice from Mylne and (Sir) John Soane, Roland Burden, an MP. and entrepreneur, adapted Paine's design for Sunderland bridge over the Wear, started in 1793 and completed in 1796. Of this Telford must have been aware when he took over from Clowes to rebuild the collapsed aqueduct over the Tern on the Shrewsbury Canal. He proposed to Jessop that same year cast iron construction for the two aqueducts on the Ellesmere Canal.

An anonymous pamphleteer commented on Paine's "patent iron bridge" (c.1792)

"The whole of our Knowledge and reasoning with respect to cast iron depends in a great measure upon judgement or conjecture with little assistance from mathematical and mechanical principals [sic]. If this is the case a man of genius and of a mechanical turn of mind may be as capable of forming a right judgement as the professional architect."[7]

This referred to Paine, Burden and Banks; the author using the term architect correctly without realisation of the new profession of Civil Engineers. Ironically, Pritchard, Mylne and Telford belonged to each, but only Mylne was leader of both. Jessop, on the other hand, adopted cast iron as a design form only after the Pontcysyllte aqueduct proved a success in 1805, whereas Telford used it thenceforth (along with masonry) for road and river bridges such as Buildwas (1795).

If he did not know Mylne personally - for he was not a member of The Smeatonian Society - Telford could not fail to have been aware of this leader of the preceding generation through his studies. As for Clowes and Jessop, Telford had worked closely with both, as he had with other colleagues, such as Dance on the London Docks (St. Katherine's) and both Rennies on the Eau Brink Cut at King's Lynn.

Back, however, to Telford's early days, particularly his association with Jessop, his superior on the Ellesmere Canal. Burton treads carefully in saying that "Charles Hadfield argues that a great deal of the credit" for the design of the astonishing cast iron trough on masonry piers for the Pontcysyllte aqueduct over the river Dee "should go to Jessop rather than Telford."[8]

The original plan by Jessop was for a series of locks down to a three-arched masonry aqueduct over the river crossing and up again whereas Telford proposed and built his high-level aqueduct without a single lock. A like situation occurred with Jessop's Grand Union Canal in the crossing of the river Ouse at Wolverton where he proposed and actually built eight temporary locks until his Resident Engineer, James Barnes, by-passed these with a cast iron aqueduct in 1802. No doubt Jessop, as Barnes' superior, should claim credit for this also. Notwithstanding Jessop's undoubted achievements as a Canal Engineer he lacked imagination and was unprepared to adopt new techniques.

In 1802, such was his increasing fame as innovative engineer, Telford, having now found his metier, was appointed by the Treasury Commissioners - again under Jessop, now ailing - to design and construct the Caledonian Canal in Scotland. By its very nature of linking lochs with canal sections to form a ship canal from east to west to cut short the sea route around the Pentland Firth, this project owed its inception to the now moribund Gloucester and Sharpness Canal, with a difference. It was funded by the Government.

Consequently it was only natural - due to the success of the Caledonian Canal, 1803-22, - that Telford should have been appointed technical advisor to the Exchequer Loan Commission in 1817 to determine the viability of completing the Gloucester and Sharpness Canal, lying idle and incomplete after some twenty years. Hence his report in 1817 urging immediate fulfilment.

The new "Resident Engineer", Upton, had been succeeded as Clerk to the Company by Phillpots, superseded in turn by Capt. Shadrach Charleton in 1820. Crawford asserts "Contemporaries and later writers agree that all the early surveys of the line of the canal were inaccurate or rushed, leading to many later difficulties"[9] listing blandly Whitworth, Clowes, Hall, George Bentley (?), Bevan and, of course, Mylne.

Crawford's assertion fails examination and compounds errors made by "later writers". No proof exists of contemporaries, other than the Berkeley clique, attacking the quality of "early surveys of the line" as inaccurate or rushed. Mylne did criticise, however, the line, fixed by the Company, to which he had to adhere on appointment as Chief Engineer. This line too was criticised by Upton, hardly a contemporary, over twenty years later.

The only rushed "survey"; if it can be termed such, was Mylne's checking of Pinnell's 1792 survey in order to obtain the Act of Parliament within three months between January and March 1793; itself no mean feat.

Crawford's list of surveyors is suspect too. George Bentley defies research and Whitworth never made a full survey let alone an early one. As stated, immediately after the Act had been passed in March 1793, the Company invited Whitworth, Mylne and Jessop - all three - to re-survey the line prior to appointing one of them Chief Engineer. Only Mylne agreed to do so.

"Later writers" inferred Mylne was, therefore, the third choice of the Company. Not content with this slur, Mylne's estimates were ridiculed by false comparisons with the ultimate cost of the canal when opened, thirty-four years later. On a like basis, Jessop's Grand Junction Canal estimates can be mocked, for the expense of keeping it open for trade proved crippling.

As for surveys, few canal projects can have been examined so often, by so many. Up to 1793 there were no less than three; two by Clowes and that by Hall and Pinnell. Mylne made five, with estimates for each apart from his "rush" one for the Act, followed by Crosley and Dadford, between 1793 and 1795.

Crawford, likewise, mentions "some distinguished engineers [who] produced schemes - for completion" before Upton's Report of 1815. They too had to survey part of the line. First came Walker, then Bevan, then Hodgkinson on behalf of Jessop and, finally, Rennie.

After Upton, Telford made one or more surveys on behalf of the Exchequer Loan Commission from 1817 on. No doubt Woodhouse, his first Resident Engineer, and his successor, Fletcher, made their own surveys and checked levels. So all in all this canal was surveyed some eighteen or more times and there is no evidence that any of these were rushed.

At this time Benjamin Bevan, an "engineer" from Leighton Buzzard, together with Henry Provis another "engineer" were, so it seems, assistant "Resident Engineers" (or Clerks of Works) to James Barnes the "famous illiterate" Resident Engineer of the Grand Junction Canal, all working to Jessop. The main task of Bevan and Provis was to measure the works as Barnes, for obvious reasons, could not do this. No wonder Jessop's estimates proved fantasy compared with final costs.

In 1804 Jessop's brick aqueduct at Wolverton on the Grand Junction caused anxiety during construction yet was opened in 1805. Three years later it collapsed; the contractors being blamed. Rennie made a report and, maybe, suggested cast iron to replace the failed masonry. Other cast iron aqueducts were inspected, including Pontcysyllte, before the new aqueduct was built in this material. So much for Hadfield's contention that Jessop rather than Telford instigated the Pontcysyllte design.

Bevan had to deal with further problems at Apsley on the Grand Junction and Telford, not Rennie, had to solve these. No wonder Mylne declared the Grand Junction to be "in a dreadful state" in 1802. (See Appendix i.) Jessop too had his share of outside scrutiny.

To assist Telford with his initial report Upton, with Company approval, sent "him plans by coach". These could only have been Mylne's set of drawings, plans, sections and details for the entire works (as recorded in his Journals), with the exception of that for the Severn Lock from Gloucester basin. They form no part of what is known as 'Telford's Atlas' i.e. his own collection of drawings rescued after his death, so Mylne's must be presumed destroyed or lost. There can be little doubt that Telford's recommendations of viability of the Canal stemmed from possession and study of Mylne's voluminous opus.

Telford's breakdown of his estimate of £125,723 to complete the canal vindicates those of Mylne if his figure of £7,000 spent on the works to his dismissal, is accepted as against the £100,000 claimed by Upton when Dadford suffered the same fate.

The breakdown of Telford's estimate is instructive:

New Works	£86,000
Land and damages	£13,872
Contingencies and Expenses	£10,651
Repairing old Canal	£15,000

In spite of a discrepancy of an odd £200, Telford reckoned £110,723 for actual completion. Set against Mylne's 1794 estimate of £121,529 (or £121,329) with but £7,000 actually spent by 1798, Telford's figure in 1817 for completion, plus that already spent, amounts to less than Mylne's original estimate of twenty three years earlier, even allowing for rampant inflation.

If Upton's figure of £100,000, spent by 1799 when Dadford was dismissed, is accepted then the total becomes £210,723 for the whole works by 1817 - a more realistic figure probably. But how could Dadford have spent £93,000 on five and a half miles canal construction within a year unless the answer is corruption on a gigantic scale. Perhaps this is why Dadford was never heard of again.

Maybe Mylne, before his dismissal, was unaware of Dadford's dishonesty hence his misconception that only £7,000 had been spent to that date. If so, suspicion has to be levelled too at the Canal Company for its own control of affairs and finances. There can be little doubt that Trye's group was involved in shady dealings.

Upton now approached his nemesis. A dispute between him and one of the contractors, concerning inferior workmanship late in 1818, made the Loan Board suspicious and loath to make further advances. Telford, as busy as Mylne and Jessop before him, took several months to investigate. In doing so, in late March 1819, he detected Upton's Achilles heel, in buying materials irregularly. Crawford intimates these were used

> "to build Saul Lodge at Frampton-on-Severn, which was to be nicknamed 'Upton's Folly' and afterwards [to be] used as the Resident Engineer's headquarters and engineering workshop."[11]

Upton resigned.[12]

He was replaced by John Woodhouse who, long before, had been part of Jessop's team on the Grand Junction Canal. He lasted no more than a year, after a fracas with Telford concerning the Sharpness seawall. Telford declared his "confidence in Woodhouse" had been destroyed and, with Upton and innumerable previous Resident Engineers in mind - not least Edson and Dadford - made a profound statement.

> "I am of the opinion that it is **absolutely necessary** to employ a Resident Engineer wholly unconnected with contractors for Materials or Labour in any shape."[13]

This was an echo of Mylne's view of Jessop and Dadford as being "without extended honour". Nor was Mylne alone in being considered "cantankerous" for Woodhouse complained at one point:

> "Mr Telford was so much out of Humour that he would not allow any explanations to take place."[14]

Woodhouse continued in office until March 1820 when he was replaced by Thomas Fletcher later that year, on Telford's personal recommendation, for they had been closely associated previously on the Chester and Ellesmere Canals.

Costs increased inevitably and a further Act had to be obtained in spring 1821 to enable further subscriptions to be raised. Meanwhile all work ceased because "the workmen had not been paid for twenty weeks and thought that the Government should be asked to take over." Indeed in early 1821, "the last loan instalment had not been repaid and the Loan Board [determined] to take over, mortgaging the Canal Company to recover the debt."[15]

Months went by during which the works silted up as previously. Telford even had to loan Fletcher money owed to him in arrears. At the end of 1821 the Loan Commissioners foreclosed[16] and took over the works; for nine months all stood idle, with disgruntled operatives remaining unpaid. Furthermore Telford was too busy - as Mylne before - to spend enough time on such matters.

NOTES

1. Thomas Telford. Brian Bracegirdle and Patricia H. Mills, 1973. David and Charles.
    An exception is "Thomas Telford's Temptations" by Charles Hadfield. M and M Baldwin. 1993. "Charles Hadfield, intrigued by discrepancies between the 'Life of Thomas Telford, Civil Engineer, written by himself and the facts, presents the theory that, Jessop, as Telford's superior, designed Pontycysyllte and Chirk aqueducts and so needs recognition as an innovator of cast iron design.
2. The Canal Builders. Burton. 1972. Eyre Methuen.
3. This term referred not to itinerancy but to the value of one day's work.
4. Designed by Clowes.
5. Ibid. 2.
6. Arch Bridges and their Builders 1735-1835. Ted Ruddock. 1979. Cambridge University Press.
7. Ibid. 6.
8. Ibid. 2.
9. Thomas Telford and the Gloucester and Berkeley Canal. G. Neville Crawford. Industrial Archaeology Review X1.2. Spring 1989.
10. The Grand Junction Canal. A. H. Faulkner. 1972. David and Charles.
11. Ibid. 9.

12. He later designed and built the Sebastopol fortress, settled there and married a Russian girl.
13. Ibid. 9.
14. In this connotation, Hadfield's contention that Jessop was sweetness and light with all contractors assumes a more sinister aspect.
15. Ibid. 9.
16. Indicating yet again the Company's mismanagement.

7

WEATHERING THE STORM

"Contentions, jealousies and prejudices are stationed like gloomy sentinels from one extremity of the line to the other but ... an honest man might look the Devil in the face without being afraid."
(Thomas Telford. 1793.)

In September 1822, the Canal Company obtained a further loan and a "national contractor", McIntosh of London, had tendered to complete the works, prompting Fletcher to inform Telford:

"I hope now, as the time is near at hand when things are likely to be improved, to be able to weather the storm."[1]

Like Mylne previously, Telford was urged to make more site visits. As late as spring 1823 Fletcher complained again that

"unless the servants are regularly paid at the proper time and properly treated they cannot perform their duties with exertion and cheerfulness."

He included himself.

By this time the Canal Company, perhaps prompted by Telford or William Holden of the Loan Commission Board, had appointed a salaried Chairman, Capt. George Nicholls. In November 1823 he asked Telford to attend a meeting to discuss the extension of Gloucester basin "as they now had possession of Smith's land" adding that "a resolution is now awaiting your arrival at the King's Head; it would have been forwarded to you had your habits been less migratory."[2] Shades of Mylne here, but as Telford held the purse strings, he received more deference.

That same month the dam holding back the Cam feeder collapsed, flooded the new works and caused a considerable setback. Some eighteen months later, in April 1825, Nicholls complained still of delays as little had been done either at Sharpness or to Gloucester basin. Fletcher, however, more concerned with the junction with the Stroudwater Canal, sent Telford a sketch proposing a variation to the original crossing involving a short new section to the latter, a new lock and stop gates. The Stroudwater Company approved this.

He also reported that McIntosh, now assured of payment, was "eagerly engaged in making arrangements to proceed more expeditiously." Telford's choice of Fletcher as Resident Engineer had been wise.[3]

Fletcher, in working to Telford at all times, upset Chairman Nicholls who was ostensibly his employer. It was a tricky situation which, after a momentary fracas, was resolved. Meanwhile costs rose alarmingly, many due to extras such as enlarging the Gloucester Basin, making the Cam feeder navigable for smaller craft with a wharf at Cambridge, varying the junction at Saul, and extending all bridge abutments against possible collision damage, quite apart from various disasters, slow progress and delays in payment with subsequent strikes. Yet Fletcher coped with them all.

The year of 1824 brought further problems, made worse by severe autumnal rain to flood the works causing confusion and the need for constant pumping. Completion seemed as far away as ever. Yet early the following year, Nicholls, on behalf of the Company sought Telford's backing for "a newly promoted canal between Gloucester and Worcester [for which] the subscription list had been filled and the only stipulation that Nicholls made was that it should be in Telford's hands."[4]

Surprisingly Telford was enthusiastic and encouraged this connection with the Birmingham and Worcester Canal. Clearly there was no limit to the leaping ambition of all concerned: this at a time of crisis, yet again, in the fortunes of a canal less than twenty miles in length. A new Bill for a further £50,000 had been submitted for approval, subject to Telford's ratification, to the Loan Commissioners prior to that of Parliament. The astonishing figure of £430,000 had now been spent, always remembering Telford's 1818 estimate of £125,723 compared with Mylne's estimate of some £123,500 a quarter of a century previously.

Why, one may ask, have Canal historians excoriated Mylne for gross underestimation if Telford did likewise? In Telford's defence, the expenditure during his control must have included interest payments on the loan to the Commission, though presumably dividend issues had ceased.

In March 1825 the dam at Sharpness, to keep out the river, just built by McIntosh, was swept away "by a tide 33ft [10m] high, measured from the lock sill."[5] Another dam at nearby Dinmore Pill collapsed and, soon after, the south river wall of the Sharpness basin was overturned by another high tide - reflecting the Gloucester basin debacle in 1798.

Labour problems for McIntosh followed and, by August, he confessed that the contract time must be exceeded, even though the proposed new lock at the mouth of the Cam feeder canal - an extra - had been excavated ready for the masonry.

Telford, after inspecting the whole works, made yet another report. In this he presaged completion to be in June 1826, six months beyond the contract date, excusing this as

> "due to difficulties regarding quarries, roads, landing places etc., and to the unprecedented changes - in **the prices** of materials and labour - [and to] the far from perfect state of the old canal when it was emptied."[6]

Further problems ensued, reported by Fletcher to Telford on 7th October 1825, including a complaint by George Hawker, Clerk of the Stroudwater Canal, that floodwater was draining into his canal. At Christmas that year, Nicholls, Fletcher and McIntosh agreed between them the impossibility of making "a perfect finish" during the winter months.

Promises of completion continued all through the following year; each time proved fallacious so dogged by persistent problems was the canal. That year the Canal Company wished to build the first warehouse at Gloucester Dock and asked Telford to design it but, considering this to be premature and being too busy anyway, he declined. Ever optimistic, the Company then appointed William Clegram as Harbour Master and General Superintendant.[7] 'Thus began a very long association with the Clegrams, father and son, with the Canal" prompting Fletcher to inform Telford in January 1826

> "I have now put Mr Clegram in possession of everything that is necessary to enable him to take charge of the works."[8]

This also proved premature for Fletcher remained another year, whereas Telford ceased his supervisory role in 1826, on becoming Consultant Engineer to the Ulster Canal Company, leaving Fletcher to oversee final completion.

In August that year the permanent connection with the Stroudwater (and Thames and Severn) Canal was made and trade burgeoned. Problems still proliferated, especially with McIntosh and landowners claiming additional recompense, but completion was set for November, then December. Telford warned that it was vital "every essential part ... be well proved before it is attempted to lay the works open to the tide water as any undue haste in this matter may be productive of very injurious consequences."[9]

At last all was virtually ready, so much so that, in mid-February 1827, the Gloucester Journal declared:

> "We have at length the satisfaction to announce that the Engineer has reported the great and important undertaking is in a state of completion and in a very few days will afford a sufficient supply of water through the entire line to promote the perfection and stability of the work."

The Gloucester and Sharpness Canal finally opened two months later, on 26th April 1827. Festivities accompanied the first vessels to ply the line entering Sharpness to guns and bells ringing and, on arrival at Gloucester, with bands playing, viewed by many thousands on the dockside. 'The Canal Committee joined the procession at the Stroudwater junction."

So thirty-four years after Robert Mylne obtained the Act of Parliament, this magnificent but ill-fated venture achieved fruition. As envisaged originally, it proved commercially viable for well over a century, but few concerned regarded it as a good investment: they only had themselves to blame.

During the Upton period, the years of stagnation, a modicum of trade evolved around the basin which, though opened in 1799, had been curtailed in size with quay walls only to the north and west. By 1824, with completion of the canal no longer in doubt, the basin was drained to remove accumulation of silt at which point a decision was made "to build a quay wall along the east side of the basin and to construct a separate Barge Basin to the south east"[10] on Samuel Playne's rope walk.

Problems arose in draining, as the basin base was lower than the river, and required pumping; the amount of silt there, and along the original five mile cut, proved formidable. The year's delay in re-watering caused disruption to trade for which compensation was demanded.

The Barge Basin was completed in one year by which time the Canal Committee had set about building warehouses. With help from the Loan Commission, the first was ready for occupation early in 1827, to anticipate the arrival of the first vessel of more than 300 tons, the brig Alchymist, in August that year. From then on traffic increased and trade in Gloucester flourished.

The subsequent story of the Docks, and indeed of the Canal itself, is told by Hugh Conway-Jones in "Gloucester Docks. An illustrated History " (1988). He sums up the completion of the Gloucester and Sharpness Canal.

"The final cost was more than twice the originally authorised capital, and much of the additional money had to be raised by loans which took over forty years to repay. This burden of debt was a great handicap to the financial prosperity of the Canal Company, but it did not prevent the canal and the docks making an important contribution to the commercial life of the city. The original proprietors may have lost all their investment, but the citizens of Gloucester were to have good reason to be grateful to them."[11]

NOTES

1. Crawford.
2. Ibid. 1.
3. Telford, of course, was never "Chief Engineer" to the Canal Company.
4. Ibid. 1.
5. Ibid. 1.
6. Ibid. 1.
7. "William Clegram from Shoreham was appointed Harbour Master, Engineer and General Superintendent although Fletcher was retained to supervise the completion of the Canal." Gloucester Docks. H. Conway-Jones. Alan Sutton. 1988.
8. Ibid. 1.
9. Ibid. 1.
10. Ibid. 7.
11. Ibid. 7.

8

NAILING THE LIE

The man that hails you Tom or Jack,
And proves by thumps upon your back
How he esteems your merit
Is such a friend that one had need
Be very much his friend indeed
To pardon or to bear it.

(William Cowper)

Canal historians have dealt harshly with Robert Mylne. It is time now to set the record straight. L. C. T. Rolt[1] remained impartial in stating that the Gloucester and Berkeley Canal [sic]

> "had been in difficulties ever since it was conceived in the canal mania period -
> [and] of the many engineers who at one time or another had a finger in this
> unprofitable pie, Robert Mylne was the man chiefly responsible. There are some
> striking similarities between Robert Mylne's career and that of Telford."

Charles Hadfield, Rolt's successor, considered Mylne to be "primarily an architect". As biographer of William Jessop he never forgave Mylne's suspicion of Jessop's probity, lashing out at him in an inaccurate account of the Gloucester and Sharpness Canal.

> "When owing to careless surveying or faulty supervision the money ran out, the
> unfortunate proprietors were compelled to go on finding money to finish the
> canal, or all that they had already invested would be worthless."[2]

Facts belie this version entirely; too late, however, to prevent subsequent historians from aping Hadfield. Take Gladwin and White.[3]

> "Robert Milne [sic] took on rather more work than he could cope with, and was
> dismissed with regularity. An ebullient man, he promptly took up some other
> position."

Weaver follows suit politely, as does Stimpson who maintained that Mylne "had little canal experience". Household accuses Mylne of pique and assumes incorrectly that Mylne proposed the Bristol and Cirencester Canal. Even G. Neville Crawford[4] observes

> "Contemporaries and later writers agree that all the early surveys of the line
> were inaccurate or rushed leading to many later difficulties."

He lists these, adding that

> "Robert Mylne was too busy to visit the site and persisted in a route to Berkeley
> Pill against his own better judgement."

He does allow Mylne some latitude for "attending Committees in the Houses of Parliament".

Hadfield concedes that all Consultant Engineers were overworked - Brindley died prematurely because of this - and excuses Jessop's shortcomings in this respect: Telford proved no exception as we have seen. So why pick on Mylne for the difficulties and shortcomings that beset the Gloucester and Sharpness Canal?

After the Act for the Canal had been passed in March 1793, Mylne had no intention of further involvement due to pressure of other business affairs. This is why the Canal Committee wrote to Jessop, **not** to appoint him Chief Engineer but to re-survey the line. Jessop was so stretched that he failed even to answer. Whitworth was then approached but had the courtesy to decline for the same reason.

A re-survey of the line was of paramount importance to shareholders unhappy with the Committee's decision to terminate the Canal at Berkeley, rather than Sharpness as Clowes had intended. Deduction now suggests that Lord Berkeley desired the Canal to pass through his land no doubt with contractual benefits, amongst which would be an arm to a basin in the town. It suggests too that Grazebrook, Trye and Lysons were part of this deal. Upton hints at such a conspiracy.

Shareholders, Loveden to the fore, insisted upon a Chief Engineer with Mylne the obvious choice. In this they prevailed but underestimated the machinations of the "Berkeley" clique with dire results to them, Mylne and the Company, for Mylne was required to adhere to Pinnell's line. Here is the paradox. Why did Mylne allow himself to be forced into such an untenable situation at this stage in his career? But once appointed Mylne lost no time in setting about his new commission. In sixteen days from 14th September to 1st October 1793 there was nothing cursory about his activities on behalf of the Canal and his new clients. So much so that the likes of Loveden and others ceased to worry further, little realising the bomb that they had now primed.

* * * * *

Before leaving for Gloucester in mid-September, Mylne had had a busy summer "on the affairs of the Western Canal". He was in Devon and Somerset most of July; Topsham, Exeter, Cullompton, Wellington, Taunton, Bridgewater, Bristol and Bath. On 30th July he "sent a long report on the Grand Western Canal with many calculations and estimates therein [sic] and soundings etc. - strictures on the Exeter and Taunton Navigation, and the Somerset Canal, Whitworth Plans etc."[5]

In August he was inspecting the Thames from Windsor downstream which led, on 26th, to his appointment "jointly with Mr Whitworth, engineer thereto" by the "Committee of the Canal Company from Taplow to Isleworth." On 10th September, after a further survey, he "settled the line of the Canal" and on his way to Gloucester "called on Mr Loveden at Fairford."[6] Was this the man "with little canal experience", the man "primarily an architect", the third choice as Chief Engineer of the Gloucester and Berkeley Canal?

It is clear that Mylne had been appointed Chief Engineer of what was called 'The London Canal' to Isleworth with Whitworth as Executive Engineer rather than "jointly" - as Mylne modestly notes - for he then declares bluntly, with no reference to Whitworth, that he "settled the line". All this before Mylne even left for Gloucester; but what after his return? With Whitworth he "surveyed different lines for the Isleworth Canal" and wrote "a report on the Middle Line". Note that Mylne, not Whitworth, wrote the report. The Taplow - or rather Maidenhead - to Isleworth Canal was one of two proposals in opposition to the Braunston to London Canal which had been projected by a group of entrepreneurs, based on Northampton, headed by the Marquis of Buckingham, and backed by the Earls of Clarendon and Essex. Later called the Grand Junction Canal (now the Grand Union), it was a bold move to circumvent the long route, via the Oxford Canal and the Thames, from the Midland industrial centres to London.

Even though the state of the river Thames caused so many problems for both the Thames and Severn and the Oxford Canal Companies, the proposed Grand Junction would cause a serious loss of trade to the Oxford and also to the Thames. So the Oxford Canal Company countered the threat with a scheme for a new cut from Hampton Gay (Thrupp) via Aylesbury and Wendover to Harrow, whereas the Taplow to Isleworth project was backed by a group headed by the Duke of Northumberland of Syon Park, Isleworth. The Grand Junction won the day and obtained its Enabling Act one month after the Gloucester and Sharpness, in April 1793: Jessop was appointed Chief Engineer.

Mylne then went to Norfolk for a week in mid-October on the matter of the Eau Brink Cut to the Ouse above Kings Lynn for which he was Chief Engineer. He records correcting "Map and noticed Hodkinson's [sic] errors." This major project for Fen drainage - shades of Cornelius Vermuyden a century before - had a history much like that of the Gloucester and Sharpness Canal in that it was completed after Mylne's death and credited to Rennie.

Hadfield manages to infer that Jessop, as ever, be credited with this major, if insufficient, drainage scheme whereas his contribution was yet another of Smeaton's "cast-offs" handed over to Jessop, his erstwhile apprentice. Much is made by Hadfield of what was, in effect, a minor matter of constructing a new sluice at Knights Gool, carried out, inevitably, by John Pinkerton, for wherever Jessop went so did he. It was completed in 1785 but, five years later, Jessop had to make further improvements by steam pumping from a drain alongside the course of the river Ouse, without thought of the by-pass cut proposed later by Mylne - the Eau Brink - in 1791.

Jessop acted on behalf of the "Marshland Proprietors" in **opposition** to the Eau Brink

Bill 1793-1795, just as Mylne did later in 1800-5 against the Grand Junction Canal. The Eau Brink Cut came to fruition finally in 1818-21 but Hadfield maintains desperately that Jessop's steam engines would have been more economical.

The remainder of 1793 saw Mylne busy with the London Canal, the New River Company business as their engineer, the Stationers' Company Estate as surveyor and architect, and a survey of the "Fleet Ditch Sewer with Lewis, Dance, Cockerel [sic] and Wyatt." He was not exactly idle. Not even Whitworth nor Jessop could claim greater demands upon their time. Yet, within this period, Mylne sent his clients a detailed drawing of the proposed lock from Gloucester basin to the river Severn, the first of many such drawings for the construction of the Canal.

The idea that Mylne "sat at his ease in London" doing nothing as claimed by the "Berkeley" clique is risible, a mere excuse for the malicious impeachment of him by Trye and Lysons that followed. Upton, treading softly, makes this abundantly clear.

The lock drawing is positive proof of Mylne's expertise, especially as he had bored 24ft down before deciding on footings at 16ft for a wall 5ft thick. The disaster, whereby Dadford neglected to close off an open culvert to the river, was caused by flood waters getting behind the unfinished wall, without proper backfilling; no wonder the wall collapsed. Yet as Upton[7] hints, the clique was intent on impeaching Mylne for the disaster. But what prompted Mylne to vilify Jessop as he did in 1802?

It cannot be dismissed as the venom of a cantankerous old man - even though Mylne was 68 on penning that fateful letter - fateful in that it destroyed his reputation, subsequently. Nor was Jessop a stripling at 57, besides which these two men had known one another for nearly thirty years as fellow members of The Smeatonian Society. On many a project they had been thrown together, admittedly often in opposition.

Had not Mylne, a founder and first Vice-President of The Smeatonians, expressed the view that "they often met accidentally in the Houses of Parliament and in the Courts of Justice, each maintaining the propriety of his own designs without knowing much of each other", adding pertinently "thus the sharp edges of their minds might be rubbed off, as it were, by a closer communication of ideas, no ways naturally hostile."?[8]

Yet, unless a monstrous hypocrite, Mylne thirty years on describes - no, accuses - Jessop of being "without any sense of extended honour." Harsh words indeed; libellous too, so not written lightly.

What proof could Mylne have had of Jessop's dishonesty? We shall never know, of course, but grounds for suspicion exist, provided by Hadfield and Skempton.[9] The Pinkerton family is involved.

* * * * *

Hadfield mentions five Pinkertons, most of them brothers so it would seem, John being the eldest. They operated as Canal Contractors over a period of thirty-seven years from 1768 to 1805. The list of some of their contracts is given in Note 16 to this chapter. Of eleven known contracts, Jessop was involved with seven in one capacity or another.

In 1791, Jessop's drawings for the Leicester Forest Navigation were co-signed by George Pinkerton, John's nephew, in his role as a "common canal cutter." Two to three years later the Pinkerton firm was busy cutting the Barnsley Canal under William Jessop as Chief Engineer.

Why then did George Pinkerton apply for the post of Resident Engineer to the Gloucester and Sharpness Canal in 1794, unless convinced of appointment by recommendation of Jessop whereby, in such a role, he could benefit the family firm which had already tendered for a contract of canal cutting? The inference of intended corruption here is blindingly obvious. Unfortunately for George and the family, Jessop and the "Berkeley Clique" recognised the impossibility of so open a backing to this end, for Mylne could not have countenanced this.

Yet Mylne must have been aware of the danger, so his strong opposition can have hardly endeared him to the like of Trye and Lysons, let alone Jessop himself. As it was, Mylne could not prevent a contract with the Pinkerton firm being ratified. So one way or another the Pinkerton-Jessop combine had achieved its object, with the inevitable law suit for extras claimed subsequently in 1802.

Jessop's involvement with the Pinkertons went back many years.

> "The late 1770s saw Jessop seemingly not sure whether he wanted to be solely an engineer, or **also** an entrepreneur in partnership with the Pinkertons. When making the Mirfield Cut[10] with John in 1776 he must have thought the neighbourhood had possibilities, for within a few years the two had started three businesses there, lime-burning, a colliery and a dry-dock. Jessop's interest in the first two lasted until about 1791, **in the last to 1800**. With James and Robert Pinkerton, he also tried his hand **at casual contracting,** when they built a section of the broad Chester Canal between the head of Beeston Brook Lock and Nantwich, together with the basin there, early in 1779."[11]

By then Jessop had been a member of the The Smeatonians for six years and had introduced John Pinkerton as a member in 1777. Thus Mylne knew of their activities as he did of their next joint venture, in 1785, when their tender for constructing the Dudley Tunnel was accepted by the Dudley Canal Company. Two years later the Pinkerton-Jessop company had to abandon the project because the Canal Company ceased payment (for reasons unstated by Hadfield and Skempton) and so forfeited £2,000 of a £4,000 bond.

Then there was the matter of tokens, issued by the Pinkerton firm, when short of money, to gullible subcontractors, suppliers and navvies. A substitute for legal coins, but worth much less than face value, these tokens could be exchanged for specified goods at specified shops or for other payments in lieu of actual money. This device, without sanction of the government, was open to considerable abuse. Hence its adoption by the Pinkerton firm; there can be no doubt whatsoever that Jessop was party to this form of fraud, if only as a "sleeping partner" in the firm.

A Pinkerton token "value one shilling" – a considerable sum then – for the Basingstoke Canal dated 1789 exists still at the National Waterways Museum, Gloucester. Hadfield blithly confirms that "Jessop seems to have agreed (sic) the contract made in October 1788, with John Pinkerton and is therefore likely to have looked over the survey and advised on the layout of the works. The canal opened in 1794." As Pinkerton's partner, Jessop's agreement of the contract figure and the use of tokens must have proved advantagous to both.

But then canal companies too were not averse to such practice. Conway-Jones refers to, and illustrates, a Gloucester and Berkeley Canal Company "trading **token** halfpenny issued for local use in 1797 during a scarcity of small change." As stated the scarcity was much more than just short-change – bankruptcy loomed – so any recipient of such a token was short-changed indeed. Who better to realise this than Robert Mylne, with the added irony that his many estimates often included a final halfpenny, bringing subsequent mockery by later canal historians?

The Grand Junction Canal Company was extolled by Hadfield as "in its heyday the greatest canal company south of Birmingham. Peers, members of the House of Commons, bankers, sat on its board, the influence of whom - extended far beyond the board room". It has also been accused of malpractice, so no wonder its Chief Engineer, Jessop, followed suit as a nympholept of financial gain.

Stanley Holland[12] reveals "underhand dealings on the part of the apparently upstanding Grand Junction Canal Company." These involved a Quaker merchant of china and glassware who rented a wharf on the Paddington basin (opened July 1801) in the summer of 1808. Thenceforth, he suffered criminal victimisation involving eviction, theft, destruction of goods and buildings, bodily harm and even imprisonment over four years. Despite action at law, he never gained redress. "He had been a lamb wandering amongst tigers and they had torn him to pieces". Nor was he the only victim.

Augustus Cove, such was his name, achieved justifiable revenge which, as Quaker, must have cost him dear. He had a copper token struck which has survived, like its counterparts, as evidence of malfeasance by canal companies, their proprietors, engineers, contractors and other servants. On it he had inscribed

> "Beware of the Grand Junction Canal Company, some of whose fraud, oppression, perjury, forgery and robbery are set forth in Augustus Cove's publications ... to be had of the booksellers."

Jessop and the Pinkertons retained close links for thirty years or more, during which time the one became a busy canal engineer, the others the largest national canal contractors. They worked together on at least seven navigations and also Rye Harbour. "John was the Pinkerton whom Jessop best liked and **trusted**" observes Hadfield before making a telling revelation. As early as 1777, when Jessop was 30,

> "with the Selby [Canal] line nearly finished we find [John] Gott [the Resident Engineer] being given the job of keeping the construction accounts,'**except that Mr Jessop Disburse the money to Mr Pinkerton and settle his accounts with him'.**"[13]

The record of the Pinkerton firm proved a sorry one. Apart from the Dudley Tunnel fiasco, it was dismissed for lack of manpower and capital by the Leicester Navigation, and abandoned the contract for the Sussex Ouze Navigation after grossly underestimating the tender. This was far from all.

Burton[14] reports the Lancaster Canal Company having "a running battle with many of their contractors, but Pinkerton and Murray were very much at the top of their black list." Gregson, Clerk of the Canal Company, wrote to Rennie, the Chief Engineer, on 11th January 1796

> "Mr Pinkerton had an idea of creating some confusion and bustle amongst us and made a speech for that purpose. Dr Rigby answered him in the way he deserved and concluded with saying that what Mr Pinkerton had advanced were palpable falsehoods. The whole of the Proprietors of Lancaster knew Mr Pinkerton was making false statements from their knowledge of the work round Lancaster. No-one seconded him - this I hope will be our closing scene with these **worthy** contractors."

Jessop himself ran into trouble on the Barnsley Canal. Pinkerton had again abandoned the contract before completion and then brought an action to claim extras in 1805. According to Hadfield 'The Master of the Rolls ... was critical of Jessop's conduct in 1793 and 1794 and stated: 'he unfortunately has fallen into a mistake with respect to the nature of the Situation in which he was placed.' Nor did the Master of the Rolls approve 'this notion of Mr Jessop's that the Company could set all to rights by that Liberal Discretion which he took for granted they would at all times exercise'."[15] To this Hadfield comments, insouciantly, that "Pinkerton comes best out of an episode that must have given Jessop much pain."

The truth of the matter is that the Pinkertons made a habit of gaining contracts with low tenders and then claiming extras. Jessop was a party to this and Mylne knew it, for he noted in his Business Journal for 1798:

> "20th July. Gloucester Canal. Wrote a long letter to Mr Wheeler on a law suit about Pinkerton's contract."[16]

What with the Berkeley 'Clique', the Pinkerton-Jessop combine, Edson and Dadford, all with sticky fingers in the pie, no wonder it proved unprofitable to the likes of Loveden, Fendall and other shareholders, including Mylne.

NOTES

1.   The Inland Waterways of England. L. C. T. Rolt. Allen and Unwin. 1950. 4th Impression 1966.
2.   British Canals. Charles Hadfield. Phoenix House. 1950.
3.   Gladwin and White. English Canals. Part II. c.1970.
4.   G. Neville Crawford.
5.   Mylne's Journals.
6.   Ibid. 5
7.   Upton. Observations. 1815.
8.   The Smeatonians. G. Watson. 1989. Thomas Telford (Press).
9.   William Jessop. 1979. David and Charles.
10.   On the Aire and Calder Navigation in Yorkshire.
11.   Ibid. 9.
12.   Canal Coins. Stanley Holland. M & M Baldwin. 1992.

13. Ibid. 9.
14. Burton. The Canal Builders. Ibid.
15. Ibid. 9.
16. Mylne's Journals and the Pinkerton Family. Canal Contractors.

List of Pinkerton Contracts 1768-1805.

1   1768 James Pinkerton. – Driffield Navigation. Yorkshire.

2   1772 James and John Pinkerton. – Market Weighton Canal. Yorkshire.

3   1774-78 James Pinkerton. – Selby Canal. Yorkshire. Engineer - William Jessop.

4   1776 John Pinkerton and William Jessop. – Mirfield Cut. Yorkshire.

5   1779 James and Robert Pinkerton and William Jessop. – Chester Canal and Nantwich Basin.

6   1785 John Pinkerton and William Jessop. – Dudley Canal Tunnel. Warwickshire.

7   1789-94 The Pinkerton Family. – Basingstoke Canal. With Jessop as Engineer.

8   1790 James, Thomas and Francis Pinkerton. – Sussex Ouse. With Jessop as Consultant Engineer. (This was a Smeaton commission, passed on to Jessop who then appointed the contractors.)

9   1791 Francis Pinkerton. – Lewis and Laughton Land Levels with Jessop as Engineer. (Again passed on by Smeaton to his pupil as early as 1768.)

10   1791 James, George and Francis Pinkerton – Leicester Navigation with George co-signing contracts and drawings with Jessop.

11   1793/4 The Pinkerton Family – Barnsley Canal, Yorkshire with Jessop as Engineer.

12   1794 George Pinkerton applied for the post of Resident Engineer to the Gloucester and Sharpness Canal. Robert Mylne – Chief Engineer. George Pinkerton NOT appointed. (This is interesting for George Pinkerton clearly had much more experience than Denis Edson who was preferred.)

13   1796 The Pinkerton Family. - Gloucester and Sharpness Canal. Robert Mylne - Chief Engineer. Appointed "Canal Cutters" at the time Jessop reported on the canal at the insistance of the Trye/Lysons clique. Was there a link between the clique, Jessop and the Pinkertons?

14   1796 The Pinkerton Family. - Lancaster Canal. John Rennie the elder, Chief Engineer. The firm was dismissed for malpractice. Jessop was still a partner.

15   1802-1805 The Pinkerton Family was still pursuing claims for extra work done on the Gloucester and Sharpness Canal and many others. This is how it made money.

9

ASSASSINATION

"Would you believe it, Father, I have been drawn into the temptation of bribery varnished over with every symptom of politeness."
(Robert Mylne, 1760.)

Scoring points off previous sources on any subject is in poor taste unless, as in this instance, it involves the necessary and justified rehabilitation of a maligned reputation. It is impossible for any historian or biographer to have the last word: any subject invites more than one subsequent interpretation.

Then there is the matter of partiality and its concomitant, balance. Until Hadfield and Skempton's biography of Jessop - "The first definitive biography of the premier civil engineer of his day and a key figure in the Industrial Revolution" - there had only been an essay by Jack Simmons in his book "Parish and Empire. Studies and Sketches" published by Collins c.1947. Simmons pointed out that "as it is, only one account of him [Jessop] has hitherto been written: a brief memoir by a fellow engineer, Samuel Hughes, which appeared in 1844." This is curious, surely?

Considering the relative wealth of material on Jessop's contemporaries and successors, vide Samuel Smiles "Lives of the Great Engineers" in which Jessop is but a footnote, Hadfield invites, almost deliberately, contestation of his claims for Jessop. Furthermore his passion for his hero provides the evidence required to substantiate Mylne's forthright views of Jessop. Hadfield's claim, therefore, that the latter must have been "the premier civil engineer of his day" is ludicrous.

Whereas Mylne's descendants kept all his records intact, Jessop's were destroyed by his - who proved obstructive to Samuel Hughes in 1844. The reason is obvious now; there was something to hide.

Not so with Mylne and the hoard of letters, including many bitter ones from his brother to his sisters, referring to Mylne as "His Worship". Then there are the Journals covering no less than forty-eight years of business life with detailed accounts and occasional poignant entries on the loss of children, wife and close relatives. Mylne, unlike Jessop, can be read like an open book, and is revealed as a man of total integrity, albeit short-fused with the likes of Jessop.

Mylne, not Jessop as claimed by Hadfield, compiled and arranged together with Sir Joseph Banks, Smeaton's Reports for publication after the latter's death. Jessop was simply one of several subscribers on the Committee. In any case Jessop had fallen foul of Banks, his principal client for the Hornecastle Navigation, "soon after a similar fiasco on the Sussex Ouse". Hadfield maintains this to be the reason Jessop failed to be elected a Fellow of the Royal Society. More likely, Banks shared Mylne's view of Jessop's probity.

And what about this?

"With Mylne, Whitworth and Rennie he [Jessop] reorganised the Society of Civil Engineers in 1793."[1] Up to Smeaton's death in 1792, Mylne had been Treasurer and Jessop, Secretary, with but three Presidents, Yeoman, Pinchbeck and Nickalls. Smeaton was never President. In 1791 Nickalls offended Smeaton, for reasons unknown, and apologised but by this time the Society was in turmoil, with too many members described by Mylne as "workmen and artificers connected with and employed in works of engineering." Did he have Jessop in mind?

Certainly, Mylne had John Pinkerton in mind so a committee of re-organisation was appointed with Mylne, Whitworth, Rennie and, yes, Jessop as members.

The outcome of this was that "Mylne, as Treasurer, remained the sole office holder until his death in 1811, and there were no more Presidents [**or Secretaries**] for nearly fifty years."[2] Does this not suggest that Jessop, as previous Secretary, had failed to fulfil his duties, and that other members now viewed him with suspicion?

Yet Hadfield proclaims Jessop the greatest engineer of his generation, and avers his innovative technique of cast iron design on the slender basis of a partnership in the Butterley Co. Ironworks. He insinuates that, as Chief Engineer of the Ellesmere/Llangollen Canal, Jessop rather than Telford instigated the design of the Pontcysyllte Aqueduct and bemoans Telford's lack of recognition of this in the latter's autobiography.

Indeed Hadfield has pursued hagiography to such an extent as to publish a book entitled "Thomas Telford's Temptations" (1993) in an attempt to denigrate "Pontifex Maximus" in favour of Jessop.

Instances of Jessop's use of cast iron are few; railroads or tramways from 1789 on, swing bridges at West India Docks - (known to be Ralph Walker's proposition) - the Wolverton aqueduct on the Grand Junction Canal at Barnes' instigation to replace Jessop's collapsed masonry aqueduct and Hill's Bridge at Bristol Dock which collapsed, due to "neglect by superintendent" in 1806, yet on rebuilding, required "some design modifications".

Recalling that Mylne's 1774 design for a cast iron bridge at Inverary was neither built nor known and, in any case, was but a footbridge of two modest spans, Pritchard's Ironbridge of 1779 created a frisson of excitement among the engineers of the time. Yet, curiously none took up the challenge to explore the potential of this material until fifteen to twenty years later.

Were Jessop to have been "the premier Civil Engineer" of the age, as Hadfield claims, one might expect him to have pursued this novel form of construction. Instead Telford took up the challenge in 1795 with his bold design for Buildwas Bridge and the Longden-on-Tern aqueduct, both replacing former masonry constructions.

With the new docks, down river of London Bridge, being planned, the City took fright sufficiently to consider almost any proposal to obviate the insuperable obstruction the bridge had posed for centuries. A competition produced a number of designs - both Dance the younger, the City Surveyor, and Mylne (but not Jessop) made submissions, as did Telford and Douglass in partnership, for a single span 600ft. cast iron bridge, following a report by Jessop recommending narrowing the river to this extent by wharves on each bank. "The scheme, however, went no further, as the Bill met opposition in Parliament and was abandoned."[3]

Staines bridge then hit the news. A masonry construction designed by Thomas Sandby proved a failure in 1797, and was replaced by a cast iron one designed by Thomas Wilson in 1803. Within a month of being opened, fractures appeared and it was closed, to be finally replaced by a timber bridge.

Meanwhile Telford had designed and was building the Pontcysyllte aqueduct over the River Dee for the Llangollen Canal, ostensibly under the supervision of Jessop. "He probably conceived the project as early as January 1794. If so the three-span aqueduct at Longden was a convenient trial of some of his ideas."[4] And Buildwas Bridge confirmed this the next year. The Dee aqueduct, opened in 1805, proved immediately successful, remaining so ever since.

Only then did Jessop, timid of tunnels and embankments, smarting from failures of masonry aqueducts strengthened, as a last resort, by cast iron ties, try his hand with the new form of construction, shamed into it by his erstwhile "Agent" now famous for cast iron bridges. Of his two designs in this genre at Bristol, one proved catastrophic for the "Premier Civil Engineer" of the time. This was Hill's Bridge, which collapsed in 1806.

It should be remembered that Jessop, now 61, was already ailing and declining new commissions, unlike Mylne who at 76 accepted the proposal to resurvey the Gloucester and Sharpness Canal at John Disney's invitation in 1810. More to the point is Jessop's late adoption of cast iron techniques for these Bristol Dock bridges. Surely had he, as Hadfield asserts, designed the Pontcysyllte aqueduct he would have used cast iron subsequently, for more than just tramroads. Telford's Longden-upon-Tern aqueduct for the Shrewsbury Canal of which he, not Jessop, was principal engineer is clear proof of his innovatory use of cast iron and coincided with that for the Pontcysyllte aqueduct as well as for the Buildwas Bridge, an equally astonishing design. Of course, Telford relied upon Wilkinson and Reynolds, the ironfounders, to ensure safety and success of the concept, a fact that Jessop signally failed to do when, timidity overcome a decade later, he attempted to emulate his quondam "Agent" in the use of the same technique. Why had he not tried it before? Ruddock sums up the failure of Hill's Bridge aptly.

"Each rib [was] composed of two curved bars linked by radial bars spaced 1ft 3in. apart. The curved bars - and the radial [were] all cast together as a perforated plate, the overall depth of the rib being 2ft 4in. However each rib was formed of only two large castings, each one more than 50ft long. These were the longest castings used since the first iron bridge and almost certainly the heaviest yet used in any bridge. ... The cast iron road plates were supported on bearers carried on vertical posts rising from the arch ribs. Both the posts and the bearers were shaped in cross section, **which was a new form. Telford** was critical of arch ribs with many joints and of ribs with bars of different thickness in a single casting. ... He also criticised ... [the] vertical spandrel members because they were not made to line up with the radial bars of the arch ribs, either in direction or position."[5]

Telford also thought an arch should spring from its abutments at right angles to give an "appearance" of strength as opposed to "a crippled appearance" as in Jessop's design of Hill's Bridge of 100ft span and 15ft rise.

It is interesting too that Rennie's design of Waterloo Bridge in Masonry, completed in 1817, had proposed foundation techniques "an exact repetition of those used by Robert Mylne at Blackfriars Bridge" fifty-seven years previously. Rennie had previously adopted Mylne's elliptical arch for his Wyre aqueduct on the Lancaster Canal but for that over the river Lune, the largest all-masonry one ever built in Britain, he made bars of "rough iron" as reinforcement connected to cross ties of cast iron. In this he aped Jessop's use of iron bars in just the same positions to repair an aqueduct on the Cromford Canal. This had failed by the water forcing out the side walls and splitting the arch.[6]

In spite of clear indication of Jessop's lack of grasp of cast iron technique, his advice was actually sought on Telford's design for London Bridge **before** he had even tried, and failed, to emulate the expertise of his former "Agent". No wonder Telford made no recognition of Jessop in his autobiography. Like Mylne, he regarded Jessop a lesser man in all respects. So much for Jessop's innovative genius. Even Hadfield admits to Jessop's preference for locks over tunnels and avoidance of embankments, unlike Telford to follow. The idea of Jessop as a technical wizard is false.

Ironically too, Jessop had, at the West India Docks, a failure in 1802 to the south wall of Limehouse Basin which, incomplete, collapsed after a high tide penetrated the backing. As Mylne blamed Dadford for the like disaster at Gloucester, so Jessop blamed his Resident Engineer, Ralph Walker. Recriminations ensued "with some very improper language between them as no cordiality existed."[7] Walker was dismissed but unlike Dadford, became a Chief Engineer in his own right. So Jessop too had claws, contrary to Hadfield's claim that he was charming, convivial and never choleric. Instances abound of this whitewashing of Jessop.

If he achieved little else other than the Grand Junction Canal "engineered" by him, he would hold his place still in the history of the canal mania. But, just as Mylne never designed the Gloucester and Sharpness Canal, nor did Jessop the Grand Junction Canal nor the Rochdale, and others likewise. James Barnes set out the line which Jessop then checked and, apart from a small reduction in length north of Leighton Buzzard, approved it, and accepted Barnes' proposals for sufficient water feeders. Soon after he was appointed Chief Engineer.

For almost every canal promoted during the mania, opposers submitted alternatives and the Grand Junction proved no exception. However, even after work started under the Enabling Act, opposition continued due to a change of line. Instead of passing through Watford and Harrow it was diverted west of Watford to Uxbridge and thence to Brentford with a branch to Paddington. In so doing it had to rely upon water from the river Colne which created fierce opposition from local Millers and other threatened interests.

This group appointed Mylne to represent them, so once again he and Jessop found themselves combatants. It is significant that Alan H. Faulkner, the historian of the Grand Junction Canal, omitted, after many years research, any mention of Mylne in view of the following document in the National Records.

"Mr Mylne's report relating to the Grand Junction Canal Dec. 15th 1801. (B. XVII 1 p. to u) [together with a plan, signed twice by Mylne, of the lower reach of the Grand Junction Canal.] This plan was shown to Robert Milne [sic], Civil Engineer, at the time of his examination in Chancery on the part of the most Noble Hugh, Duke of Northumberland and others. Complainants against the Grand Junction Canal Company and the Attorney General. Defendants.

J. A. Berrey. Deputy Examiner."

The date of the Report is of vital interest for it preceded Mylne's notorious letter to Wheeler, Clerk to the Gloucester and Sharpness Canal Company, by a matter of only six weeks. And it is this report that must have prompted Mylne to make his verdict on Jessop public.

It is reproduced more or less in full (see Appendix i) together with extracts from Mylne's Journals for the same period (See Appendix ii) as evidence of Mylne's working methods, his professional relationship with Jessop and his own personality which emerges from mere words in convincing manner. No sign here of a cantankerous old man; so what did Mylne have to report on the Grand Junction Canal to his clients? Faulkner is forced to confirm all Mylne's strictures of the southern section of the canal in a chapter devoted to the problems of the "Tring and Braunston Summits".

The problems were water shortage, problems that never affected the completed Gloucester and Sharpness Canal but, to be fair, the two canals cannot be compared. Yet even today, two hundred years later, the Grand Junction (Grand Union) Canal is still bedevilled by the same problem, ever a weeping expense. And Mylne stressed this in his report.

What concerns us here are Mylne's remarks in wider context. Well into his report, he observes

"I have had occasion to be well acquainted with many portions of these rivers (i.e. the Colne Valley) during thirty-five years on the subject of disputes at law or otherwise when the interests of one stream had ... to contend against its opposite; and on a variety of projects and speculations which (fortunately for the Publick as well as individuals) were found in time to be visionary and illusive ... It is necessary to state the general result of the Inspection, namely that ... portions of the undertaking have been so **erroneously and parsimoniously executed**, it is extremely subject to failure."

Mylne then described his visit "to the summit level ... and the navigable feeder from Wendover" which he found "perfectly dry and empty" and listed means of water supply and their inadequacy, especially that of "the Wendover Reservoir - no good." He maintained rightly - as subsequently proved - this to be "a consumer by absorption and evaporation instead of a feeder." He deals with water demand and then wonders how this is to be supplied.

"All has been done which was thought necessary by their professional advisors, as appears, by the Canal having been solemnly opened as a finished work for publick use. How vain and visionary it has proved ... the whole of these hills are in substance the most dry, broken rotten stone ... which are to be found in this island and the example of Sapperton Tunnel on a distant part of these hills might have afforded a precedent for well-founded suspicion instead of unwary confidence."

It is a long report, well worth reading, for it is a rare contemporary document. Concerned with the obvious shortage of water feeders to the Canal, Mylne spotted that the canal had been constructed deliberately to pass over and obscure Gutch Well just below Batchworth Lock at Rickmansworth "to hide the deceit" and stated further

"I remember it well in its former state; I have of late had occasion to mark the **sly pleasantry** of their agents [i.e. Jessop and Barnes] on this subject when mentioned by them with no small degree of self-complaisance - I left the subject to their exultation and mention it now in this day of counting for retribution - this water belongs to the hills below Uxbridge."

He uncovers a further plot by the "agents" of the Grand Junction Canal Company to disarm the opposition (i.e. Mylne's clients) - the provision, ostensibly, of a reservoir at "Riselip" [sic] for the Millers "in lieu of water to be taken from the Colne" on the basis that this reservoir would be so ample as to "supply the needs or some needs of the Metropolis".

As Mylne remarked "If there is anywise foundation for such a thing ... it must be as a truism".

Moving towards conclusion, Mylne refers to Jessop's report to the Grand Junction Company, dated 24th October 1792, in which he refers to the anticipated water supply for the canal "based on **Mr Barnes'** measurements". and comments

> "this project has been realised in form but in respect of water it has not an existence in 1802."

The strictures on inadequate water supply to the Tring summit made by Mylne in his 1802 report bear examination if only to emphasise the inexpertise of James Barnes, the Resident Engineer, who actually planned the line in 1792. More important, Jessop as Chief Engineer must accept full responsibility for defective water supply to the summit. It will be recalled that on checking Barnes' line he made one small alteration to shorten the line north of Leighton Buzzard.

Mylne mentioned one reservoir only provided, that **below** the Marsworth top lock. This was Wilstone No.1 created in 1802, enlarged in 1811 and again in 1827. Then in 1806, Marsworth reservoir was created.

As the Tring summit pound was only three miles long and had to serve twenty-three locks to the north down to the Ouze valley, and fifty-one locks south to Hanwell, it must have been clear immediately that the Wendover feeder, however flush, could never cope with demand.

Mylne was the first to identify its deficiencies and Jessop's attempts to overcome this by filching the waters of the Bulbourne, Gade, Colne and Frays rivers without permission or compensation. Hence the frenzy of reservoir construction in the Marsworth area beyond the two considered sufficient up to 1806.

More followed. Apart from the enlargement of Wilstone No.1, as mentioned, Tringford reservoir was dug in 1816, Startopsend adjacent in 1817, Wilstone No.2 in 1836 and No.3 in 1839 - eight in all. And even these are still insufficient.

Perhaps it is just as well Jessop died in 1814 when but three had proved essential to plug this continual leak to the summit pound - and to the Grand Junction Canal Company's finances. Otherwise it might well have sought recompense for negligence from its Chief Engineer by recourse to law.

So Mylne was proved right as the history of this canal vide Faulkner confirms. Jessop had feet of clay. But he was careful for when John Pinkerton's nephew, George, applied for the post of Resident Engineer to the Gloucester and Sharpness Canal even he had to back Mylne's refusal of such an appointment. Yet that did not prevent him from reporting on Mylne's design details knowing full well that Mylne was under attack by the Trye/Lysons clique.

Hadfield makes nonsense of Jessop's report by maintaining that he "suggested" improvements (already made by Mylne) regarding line deviations and even recommended swing rather than lift bridges; it was Whitworth who suggested that lift bridges might be cheaper than swing bridges.

From Mylne's curt entries in his journal one can glean now and then a sense of disapproval of Jessop, distaste even in entries such as that for 22nd November 1800 on the Rickmansworth (i.e. Grand Junction) business "on Mr Jessop disappointing me". Jessop failed to keep an appointment.

Even on such small matters as repayment of travel expenses, paid by Mylne for Jessop on joint outings, the latter proved dilatory. Mylne conversely was scrupulous over all debts and monetary transactions, adding interest to delayed repayments of his own debts - all noted in his Journal. A mean Scotsman one might say, but Mylne had no hesitation in saving his brother, after the Edinburgh North Bridge disaster, for which he received animosity rather than gratitude.

It is unlikely that Mylne disliked Jessop as Hadfield maintains; certainly he could not have been jealous for he was after all, undisputed leader of the engineering profession after Smeaton's death.

As Mylne coupled Jessop with Dadford in the notorious letter, it seems proper to examine the role of the Resident Engineer at that time. James Dadford proves a shadowy figure. It has been assumed that he was nephew of Thomas Dadford senior.

Burton[8] mentions Thomas Dadford, of the Brecknock and Abergavenny Canal, unaware that this was Thomas Dadford junior, and supposes him to be the Dadford in Mylne's letter. Hadfield[9] lists under "Other Engineers of Note" connected with Canal Acts, John Dadford (3 projects) and Thomas junior (3 projects). John surveyed the first line of the Aberdare Canal, Thomas junior was involved with Leominster, Monmouth, Neath and Glamorganshire Canals, and, jointly with his father, Thomas senior, the east branch of the Montgomery, linking it with the Llangollen Canal. Indeed Thomas junior was an **assistant to Jessop in 1793** in surveying the line of the Llangollen. Twelve years earlier, father and son Thomas, had surveyed the river Trent, prior to Jessop's own survey of 1782.

Having been led to believe that Thomas Dadford senior was a surveyor, if not an engineer, Hadfield states that he was appointed contractor on the Cromford Canal with Thomas Sheasby - "both were old hands" - and continues

> "On the Cromford Canal between 1789 and its completion in 1794, Jessop gained more experience than he had bargained for. It must have taught him much. In January 1791 he was **caught out** by his contractors leaving the job (they went to Wales to dig the Glamorgan Canal) at a moment, **when he had overpaid** them by £1332. The money seems **not** to have been recovered, and he and Outram [Resident Engineer] decided to continue, using direct labour plus some small sub-contractors."

Now Russell[10] maintains that Thomas Dadford junior, together with John Priddey, carried out a survey of the Stroudwater Canal in 1775, yet in May that year "the first stone of the entrance lock at Framilode" was laid[11], Thomas Yeoman and Benjamin Grazebrook having already established the line.

This raises two points of interest. No exact dates exist for any of the Dadfords yet 1775 is the first mention of Thomas junior rather than his father. As minor figures, the Dadfords flit across the stage of the Canal era for a quarter century by the end of which Thomas senior must have been an old man to have reverted from Surveyor to "common canal cutter" as late as 1791.

Secondly, there must surely be some connection between Thomas Dadford junior's involvement with the Stroudwater Canal in 1775 and the appointment of James Dadford as Resident Engineer of the Gloucester and Sharpness Canal in 1795. Gladwin and White provide the only information available on Thomas Dadford junior - without source.

> "A good theoretical engineer, known for his work on Welsh Canals, but was eventually dismissed from post due to inattention to work. Was unable to control his workmen, which led to 'go-slows' and hence delays in completion. Probably took on too much work."

James Dadford must have had influential contacts to be appointed Resident Engineer without any previous or practical experience. Could Jessop have, perchance, recommended him initially before realisation of possible consequences?

Burton[12] provides insight to both Chief and Resident Engineers.

> "Once the chief engineer for a canal project had laid down his plans and drawn up his specifications he had finished the first part of his job. **He could then hand the whole lot over to the Committee and leave for the next Canal. The job of supervising the actual building of the waterway then fell to the Resident Engineer.**"

He quotes Rennie as stating that the one important difficulty to be overcome was "of obtaining Resident Engineers and Agents of **abilities, integrity** and **experience**". Burton then observes that "during the mania years, a good engineer was very much in demand". Rennie reckoned, as Chief Engineer, **only to "inspect the works before each quarterly meeting of the Company."**

Smeaton, previously, had made the point regarding Resident Engineers.

> "To fit a man fully for this employment, requires so great a number of qualifications, that I look upon it as impracticable to find them united in one person. I therefore take it for granted, that he will, of course, be materially deficient in something; and as such, there is the greatest difficulty in the world to preserve good understanding between the Resident Engineer and the Committee who directs him. His post is the post of envy. Not only all the inferior

departments are ambitious to be practical engineers, but **even members of the Committee have a propensity that way too**; by which means all become masters, and he who ought to be so, being deprived of authority, it is easy to figure the confusion that may follow."

Smeaton stressed the problem of proprietors abrogating to themselves knowledge of engineering e.g. Grazebrook on the Thames and Severn and Trye and Lysons with the Gloucester and Sharpness. In both cases Mylne made clear his scorn of such amateurs and thereby created enemies. What Smeaton failed to pinpoint was the temptation of Resident Engineers to indulge in perks of one sort or another. Edson, Upton and Woodhouse all paid the penalty for dishonesty; all credit then to Fletcher for being free of such taint. Was Jessop likewise in his dealings with the Pinkertons and Dadford?

Burton, too, is sound on the Resident Engineers' duties. Before any cutting began he had to decide what land was needed and then acquire it for the Company. He then had to **survey** it.

> "Although the Parliamentary line had already been laid down, it gave only a rough indication of the route. The final choice lay with the **resident engineer**, who had to find the best and cheapest line, taking into account both the cost of the land and the cost of cutting. The actual purchase was sometimes undertaken by the engineer, sometimes by the secretary."

Burton makes passing reference to a crucial aspect of the Resident Engineer's task, that of measuring the work completed - now termed quantity surveying - as against the Contractors' claims. This aspect tested probity and many Resident Engineers succumbed to temptations of double-dealing. Not only Resident Engineers, alas, but Chief Engineers too.

Unacknowledged by historians, Robert Mylne was much in demand as an Arbitrator thus confirming his status as leader of the Civil Engineers' profession. On 7th November 1792 he noted

> "Meeting on arbitration of dispute in Lancashire - heard council and solicitor etc - adjourned till 24th." [A week later he] "met with Mr Rennie on the business of the [Yorkshire] Ouze" [and on the 24th he] "heard further evidence on the arbitration of the Wyer [sic] (Wyre) etc. and closed the enquiry - 3. Held a conference with Mr Creasy and Rennie on the Ouze and his intended survey - 3."

On 14th December, Mylne left London for Yorkshire, via Grantham, Doncaster, Thorne, Rotherham and Sheffield, busy on surveys of various waterways.

> "Dec. 26th. Bad day in chaise to Sheffield - viewed line, lands, brooks to that place - viewed the termination and place for bason - attended a committee - made a viva voce report to the meeting on this canal - at Sheffield."

The next day he set off on the business of the Rochdale Canal. At this point the Mylne myth of obduracy obtrudes yet again in a letter from the General Manager of the Rochdale Canal Company to the author (7th May 1952).

"Dear Sir,

ROBERT MYLNE.

Regarding your letter of April 27th., the canal records indicate that in June 1791 John Rennie of London was appointed Surveyor and Engineer of the intended Rochdale Canal, and that in November 1792 Robert Mylne was retained to accompany Rennie in examining the line of canal - presumably in an advisory capacity. It then appears that Mylne, after three days examination during December 1792, insisted on leaving Manchester for Birmingham because his engagements were so heavy. This incomplete examination evidently **distressed** Rennie a good deal, and there **all reference** to Mylne ends.

Yours faithfully,

General Manager."

Now here is an example of the unwitting lie, no less pernicious for that, propagated by a canal company official. The tone of his letter is denigratory; the presumption, the statement of fact and the inference to follow, all show a clear bias against Mylne. Why so?

The reality defies such interpretation and poses a question. Who paid Mylne for his survey of the Rochdale Canal and his part in obtaining the enabling Act? Was it Rennie himself? Unlikely, but, if not, why the cessation in Company records of any later reference to Mylne and any payments to him? It is almost as if the conspiracy had started within Mylne's lifetime. The accusation of an incomplete examination is without foundation. Let Mylne, himself, put the record straight.

On 27th December 1792, he left Sheffield for Huddersfield and Halifax where he met William Crosley, a proprietor and Resident Engineer of the proposed Rochdale Canal. The next day they viewed together

> "the upper end of the Calder and the canal from Sowerby Bridge to Todmorden - and took in all the Mills on the canal, the river and line and ground of the canal at Todmorden.
>
> Dec. 29th. Viewed streams and line of canal to Rochdale.
>
> Dec. 30th. Viewed line of canal etc. to Manchester. At Manchester - surveyed canal junction and end of Bury Canal. **NO** Mr Rennie at The Swan. **Finished** the Rochdale.
>
> Dec. 31st. Left Manchester, Mr Rennie **NOT** being come. At Newcastle under Line [sic]."

Yes, Mylne did go to Birmingham to meet James Watt all day on 2nd January 1793. A week later he

> "made out and sent a list of Mills on the Calder to Mr Travis and a copy of **my plan** of the Rochdale Canal."

On 24th January Mylne set off for Gloucester to collect information for the Gloucester and Berkeley Canal Bill, returning to London on 30th January.

Five days later on 4th February he

> "Met Mr Rennie [for] consultation on the Rochdale Canal before attending the House of Commons the whole day on 2nd reading of the Bill and the Committee - not called."

It is even more curious that the Rochdale Canal Company has no record of Mylne representing it in the House of Lords on 30th March 1794 on the later bill. This prevented him from attending the Gloucester Canal Company meeting on that date (See Chapter 3). Mylne was no slouch, so how could Rennie have been "distressed - a good deal"?

It is equally curious that Hadfield and Skempton fail to mention Mylne's participation in the Rochdale Canal. They maintain that this canal, which Samuel Smiles declared to be stamped by "the mark of a master's hand", was Jessop's "unknown achievement".

> "The truth is that Rennie was much concerned with the canal promoters' two unsuccessful Bills of 1792 and 1793, less with the Act of 1794, not at all with construction. It was Jessop who wrote the crucial report that changed opinion, and he that piloted the 1794 Act through Parliament. He then **laid out the line** (which of course owed much to Rennie's previous surveys), designed the structures and from time to time inspected it while it was building."[13]
>
> A strange statement this since it was William Crosley, together with Mylne, who established the line without Rennie, late in 1792. In February 1793 Mylne spent no less than ten days on the Rochdale Canal with Rennie and proprietors. He even provided "a drawing for measuring water and an estimate of the quantity wanted".

Yet for some reason or another, at the end of it all, "declined giving evidence" in 1792. Did he smell corruption here too?

According to Hadfield & Skempton

> "Rennie seems to have had little to do with the third Bill, though the deposited plan was surveyed by Crosley under his direction."

This is a half-truth for Crosley and Mylne laid out the line. Rennie never turned up.

Mylne was present too on 30th March 1793 at the Parliamentary Committee when "Jessop was asked how much of the proposed line he had himself seen".

He replied (as Hadfield reports somewhat naively)

"I viewed the line by walking over **part** of it and seeing the other parts as I travelled along the road where there were to me no objects of particular Inquiry. The Information I received was by using my Eyes, making such Inquiry as I thought necessary on the spot..."[14]

As for water supply for this admirable canal, "with so great a rise and fall" and to protect millowners' waters Jessop's conviction was "that reservoirs of ample capacity could be built".

On the basis of this assurance and Mylne's assessment of water requirements — the obvious reason for his attendance upon the Committee — the Rochdale Act was indeed passed on 4th April. So whose was "the mark of the master's hand"? Certainly it was neither Rennie nor Jessop.

No wonder Mylne in that very year, 1794, prevailed upon Crosley to check the levels of the Gloucester and Sharpness Canal even at the expense of dragging him from Rochdale to Gloucester. No wonder Mylne noted Dadford's 3" discrepancy.

Then there was the matter of the Trent Navigation and the Nottingham Canal in April that same year. Jessop found himself, without qualm, engineer to two rival companies intent on bypassing the shallows above Trent Bridge with what is now known as the Beeston Cut.

Shareholders decided "to employ some able engineer to survey the River **along** with Mr Jessop and to report to them the most effectual means for making ... improvements".

No just one but no less than three other engineers were involved to sort out Jessop's problems. No surprise to discover that these were Mylne, Rennie and Whitworth. Somewhat surprising to find that Mylne and Rennie assessed the problem in tandem on 25th-26th April 1793 but it took another year for the Act to be passed.

The point in question is how much was Jessop forced to accede to the advice of his peers, not just in this instance, but throughout his career.

Hadfield maintains, in his hagiography of Jessop, that the chief or principal engineer should be credited with every aspect of the canal to which he was appointed. This is simply not so, as Burton makes clear and as the story of the Gloucester & Sharpness confirms.

Rarely did any Principal Engineer conceive a project, rarely did he establish the line, rarely did he supervise the work or have to account for it — all these tasks were pre-empted by proprietors and delegated to Resident Engineers.

The Principal or Chief Engineer was primarily a Consultant — an "architect" of imagination to provide expertise for the overall conception plus drawings and specifications in the light of new technology — not a supervisor. He estimated costs for completion without control over actual costs, but inevitably was held responsible for these, all problems during construction and all defects, no matter the cause. An unenviable position to hold when made the scapegoat more often than not.

Whereas Jessop thrived on the risks involved, provided the clandestine rewards proved sufficient, Mylne bridled at any hint of impropriety. Jessop, on the one hand, was — so it is said — self-effacing, modest but somewhat obsequious, Mylne on the other, as we know, was inclined to arrogance and volatility; not without reason when faced with stupidity and deviousness.

Their respective portraits clearly reveal their characteristics. It is a measure of the time that Jessop was so in demand for potentially lucrative ventures, whereas Mylne had little concern for "bags of money".

NOTES

1.   Wiliam Jessop. Hadfield and Skempton 1979. David & Charles. This should read 'The Smeatonian Society' not Civil Engineers.
2.   The Smeatonians. G. Watson 1989. Telford Press.
3.   Arch Bridges & Their Builders 1735-1835. Ted Ruddock 1979 C.U.P.
4.   Ibid 3.
5.   Ibid 3.

6.   Ibid 3.
7.   Ibid 1.
8.   The Canal Builders A. Burton 1972 Eyre & Methuen.
9.   Ibid 1.
10.   Lost Canals of England and Wales. R. Russell. 1971. David and Charles.
11.   Thames and Severn. H. Household 1969. David & Charles.
12.   Ibid 8.
13.   Ibid 1.
14.   In view of this lamentable statement, could Mylne's evidence have turned the tables to enable the Bill to be passed. Supposition but conceivable.

10

VERDICT

"The Dangers of an Honest Man in much Company."
(Abraham Cowley)

A lamentable story? No, not the conception of the Gloucester and Sharpness Canal; this was bold indeed and all credit to the entrepreneurs of Gloucester. They owed perception to Benjamin Grazebrook of Stroud who set imagination ablaze with, first, his modest Stroudwater Canal - an undoubted success - and then the extension to the Thames.

In this, his lack of engineering expertise let him down. He owed much to Clowes and Perry for his success, whereas his Bristol to Cirencester project was a will o' the wisp, stillborn by the censure of the real professional, Robert Mylne.

Nevertheless it could only have been Grazebrook who inspired those in Gloucester to follow his example by contemplating the Gloucester and Hereford Canal in 1790. Understandably Clowes, having proved his worth as Resident Engineer of the Thames and Severn, was their choice for this venture. Not for them the recognised national engineers, whatever their expertise, for they were to be had at too high a price for provincial adventurers. In any case they had had their fill of them, and their devastating reports on the Thames and Severn, accusing proprietors of ignorance and megalomania.

The fact that Clowes' work on the Gloucester and Hereford hit problems at an early stage, whether from inexpertise or incompetence by proprietors themselves in financial management i.e. issuing shares too soon, did not detract from opinion of his worth. He came cheap. So after a decade of wavering, the Gloucester adventurers had no hesitation in employing him to lay out the line of their new grandiose conception. This he did with alacrity and efficiency, fixing the terminus with the Severn at a bleak point called Sharpness.

It is my contention, unproven, that this displeased Lord Berkeley of Berkeley Castle and Berkeley town, who then insisted that the canal terminus be changed to Berkeley Pill with a branch cut to the town whatever the cost. It is my contention, too, that those Gloucester merchants bowed to his wishes and engaged Richard Hall, assistant Clerk of Works to the Thames and Severn Canal, to produce a change of line surveyed by Hall's partner in land-surveying, Thomas Pinnell. He drew up a plan dated 1792. This was circulated to subscribers, prior to obtaining an Enabling Act, and attracted a welcome response. Other local landowners through whose property the Canal was to pass, such as Dr Lysons and Mr Cambridge, were supporters, provided the line was adapted to their convenience. This was agreed.

Neither Clowes nor Hall were capable of transforming the Bill into an Act. Thus the proprietors were forced to commission Robert Mylne, the prime exponent of the time, to achieve their object. They made it clear the chosen line to Berkeley was fixed and no deviation could be entertained.

Thus it was that Mylne became involved. After he achieved their object many influential shareholders, such as Edward Loveden, insisted that Mylne be appointed Chief Engineer even though their Gloucester colleagues favoured a less expensive choice.

Mylne won the day but in doing so made enemies of Lysons, Trye and other toadies of Lord Berkeley. Hence the scene was set for a conspiracy against Mylne which, as we have seen, took its fatal course.

The Berkeley Clique assumed domination of the Canal Committee and chose the Resident Engineers, without reference to Mylne, on the basis of low salary rather than experience or expertise thereby causing the debacle to follow.

Whether they, themselves, were corrupt is open to interpretation. But Trye, Lysons and Cambridge all insisted upon variations to their own personal advantage tantamount to blackmail.

That they dominated the Canal Committee in the appointment of Resident Engineers suggests that they knew the inevitable perks asociated with the post and, no doubt, demanded a back-hander. No doubt too they expected this of the Chief Engineer likewise, thus their partiality for Jessop, said to accede to such pressures after taking his cut.

The initial adulation of Mylne was but a softener to pressure to come. Then came the shock of Mylne's integrity and so attitudes changed and the debacle was inevitable.

This the group ensured by carping constantly at Mylne, knowing full well that due to other commitments, he could never devote enough time to their concern. Consequently all problems could be laid at his door, absolving them from any accusation of intrigue, volubly denied in their impeachment of Mylne.

So successful were they that, in short time, Mylne became the scapegoat. Meanwhile, as was the custom of all such ventures, they received dividends on their initial investment and so were not entire losers thereby. The money ran out, of course, and again Mylne was blamed. And so they sacked him. Within a year their great project was moribund. All investors had lost their stake, less dividends already paid. All they had for their money was a half-finished basin and a few miles of useless cut, both of which promptly began to silt up.

Paralysed by their own stupidity, they did little but wring their hands prompting Mylne, as a shareholder, to declare in 1802

"Is there nothing going forward with the canal? Is it to lay dormant, in a deserted state for ever. It always was in want of a Chancellor of the Exchequer, and a better Chairman."

How right he was. But this was no letter of revenge. Yet why did he state categorically that the misfortunes stemmed "from the time of Jessop's visit"? Because he maintained - clearly with some irrefutable evidence in mind - that both Jessop and Dadford were "without any sense of extended honour". This was an accusation of corruption - nothing less. It has been proved that the Dadford family and Jessop himself were well acquainted, both having had rewarding experience, along with the Pinkertons, as "common canal cutters". Perhaps one might add Lysons and Trye on the supposition that their impeachment of Mylne was nothing less than disbelief at his **incorruptibility**.

Whom then did Upton finger as the proprietor intent upon completion of the canal, at any cost, to the totally inappropriate terminus at Hock Crib? Not Dr Lysons for he died in 1800, but it could have been his nephew, the Reverend topographer. More likely it was Charles Brandon Trye who had insisted that the tramroad from Gloucester Dock to Cheltenham branched to his Leckhampton Stone Quarry. Alas, even Upton proved tainted likewise, as Telford discovered.

The Gloucester and Sharpness Canal would have remained moribund but for chance; the political situation after the prolonged Napoleonic War that ended finally in 1815. Were it not for that, Telford could have played no part in the completion of the Canal.

As it was, again by chance, his role as Engineering Consultant to the Board of the Loan Exchequer Commission enabled him to recommend finance for completion. Even this took six years before the project could be revived.

From then on he became in effect "Chancellor of the Exchequer" thus by-passing control by the Canal Company, and precluding local cliques intent upon "back-handers" during construction.

No matter Mylne's high sense of morality, bribery and corruption in those days were accepted facts of life. It happened that Telford shared Mylne's conceptions of honesty and so, quite apart from their own individual brilliance - call it genius - in their "new" profession, they were a world apart from the likes of Jessop, whose main consideration was acquisition of "bags of money", deplored by Smeaton.

In Thomas Fletcher, his Resident Engineer, Telford found a man of like probity, one he could trust implicitly, one who never let him down. If credit there be in this sad moral story, Thomas Fletcher deserves the accolade for he it was who finally, in Hadfield's term, "engineered the Gloucester and Sharpness Canal" and brought it to a triumphant conclusion.

* * * * *

And that is the chronicle of this canal, a unique canal, that finally fulfilled the expectations of those who conceived it. To them, the men of Gloucester, must be given all credit for perspicacity, if nothing else. None of them lived to see what they had achieved.

What began as an investigation has ended with a serious charge against the man considered by some to be "the premier civil engineer of his day". William Jessop now stands in the dock of the Court of History indicted of what? The charge is two-fold: one, that he was corrupt: two, that his reputation as civil engineer has been misrepresented.

The prosecution witness is Robert Mylne, civil engineer; that for the defence, Charles Hadfield, Canal historian. Evidence has been submitted: time now for summation.

Ignoring Mylne and Jessop's joint experience of dock wall collapse when both blamed their respective resident engineers, Mylne had one, and one only, major failure in constructional design - the collapse of his Welbeck bridge for the Duke of Portland, early in his career in 1765.

Conversely, Jessop's two masonry aqueducts on the Cromford Canal had to be rebuilt in part and that at Wolverton on the Grand Junction, late in his career, collapsed as did his attempt at cast iron bridge design - Hill's bridge in Bristol Docks. This required design modifications on rebuilding. Then, no less than four of his six locks on the Upper Thames collapsed almost immediately.

More important still, his many canals suffered from chronic water shortage, in particular the Grand Junction (Union) Canal, considered his greatest achievement. Even today the problem continues, as confirmed by Chris Mitchell, British Waterways Assistant Engineering Manager who, in an article for Waterways World October 1992, declared that "By 1805 ... water shortages were a great problem" only overcome by extended back-pumping systems.

And had it not been for Telford, Jessop's Resident Engineer on the Llangollen Canal, making a permanent feeder from the Horseshoe Falls of the river Dee, that canal too, originally intended from Ellesmere to Chester via Ruabon would have suffered likewise.

As Hadfield makes clear Jessop, as the disciple of Smeaton, an acknowledged genius, only achieved his reputation through Smeaton. The subsequent canal mania boosted this to promote Jessop as the man of the hour in spite of his limitations.

Chance, and maybe more than chance, dictated that Jessop be so during the mania. It is more than coincidence that where he went, the Pinkertons went, suggesting a formidable "design and construct" team of great appeal to the many canal promoters clamouring to have a slice of what appeared to be such a large profitable pie.

Statistically this team figures prominently in contemporary records, leading canal historians into a trap. Thus when Mylne, guardedly, leaked a hint of impropriety he was scorned as a bitter old man, and Jessop remained the icon of the mania.

It could be said that Jessop was the Robert Maxwell of his time but avoided exposure, in spite of Mylne's clear accusation. No wonder Jessop died a wealthy man, no wonder his family obstructed Simon Hughes' innocent investigations thirty years after his death, because all incriminating papers had been destroyed.

In forming his rationale for The Smeatonian Society, little could have Mylne realised that, with Jessop, this would be put to the test; nor could he have conceived that his own reputation would be so denigrated.

Likewise, it was a matter of considerable surprise that Mylne did not die a wealthy man and caused the comment that "he loved his profession but not the emoluments of it". That speaks volumes and points the difference between him and Jessop.

Mylne and Jessop knew one another, socially and professionally, for at least thirty-five years. Why at the end of it all should Mylne speak so openly? That, members of the jury (dear readers), you have to decide. As judge (and author) I declare both charges proved. It must now be said, indeed, that Jessop was "as much inferior to Mylne as a glow-worm to the Sun"

The Gloucester and Sharpness Canal has made history in more ways than one.

Pace Robert Mylne.

Appendix i

Transcription of part of
"Mr Mylne's Report relating to the Grand Junction Canal".

Dec. 15th 1801.

To the Gentlemen met at the White Horse Inn, Uxbridge, on the 3rd Oct. 1801; interested in the waters of the rivers Colne, Verulam, Gade, Bulbourne, Chesham and Missen: and to such other persons as have property in the use and purposes for which the said rivers, their contributary streams or springs are anyways applied; either in a separate or combined state, between Tring in Hertfordshire and Staines and Brentford in Middlesex.

GENTLEMEN

Having received your resolutions appointing me to survey the Grand Junction Canal to discover and ascertain the causes of your loss of water; and the proportion of the quantity of water taken away, bears to the quantity supplied by the Canal Company; and having also received the several instructions and explanations communicated to me at another meeting held at the said place on October 20th, I beg leave to state that I applied to the making of the said survey; to the investigation of facts; to a due consideration of the operation which arises out of the Acts of Parliament under which the Grand Junction Canal has been formed; and also to the effect of those connections which have been made with your rivers, brooks and springs directly or indirectly from the period of its first formation.

At a meeting held on the 17th November at the Rose and Crown, Hounslow, I had the honour to state viva-voce and generally the result of my labours in this important business, and the effect arising from a close collected consideration of the whole.

I was heard with an attention which requires my sincere thanks: and the Resolutions come to, convey your esteemed approbation - yet as many persons could not then possibly be present - and as many more are, intimately and most seriously interested in this business without having any knowledge or even suspicion of being so, I am now to compleat [sic] what I undertook by submitting in writing the statement I made to the Gentlemen then present.

COURSE OF THE RIVERS

It is necessary to premise that the six rivers derive their sources of supply from a circle of hill country extending from the heads of the Colne near South Mimms and Bushey Common on the east round to the south side of the hills near Wendover where the valley of Missenden obtains its streams. All these are finally collected into one common head or level of water at and next above the town of Uxbridge.

There the waters are again divided into three equal portions passing through the Mills of Mr Mercer, Mr William Hull and of Mr Samuel Hull. Thence they take at first their separate courses and afterwards are varied in the most strange manner ….

Ultimately the whole fall by ten mouths to the Thames between a point opposite Egham above Staines bridge and the supply of water to Syon House, near Brentford …. Thus there appears an obvious line marked by nature in the whole of this wide-lying country being drained to the town of Uxbridge and these waters having run through that pass diverge immediately preserving different levels - and keeping courses as above stated they fall into the Thames at distances extremely wide of one another, after supplying the Royal Establishments at and around Hampton Court; several Princely mansions and manufactures of the most useful, costly and extensive kind in this country.

LINE OF CANAL.

The Grand Junction Canal passes over the long range of dry hills- east to west - at a gap or pass (the lowest no doubt which could be found thereabouts) near to Tring.

From that elevated summit (395 feet above Thames Level) the line of the Canal from the north passes through Berkhamstead down the valley of the Bulbourne and falls … 124 feet nearly till it joins the valley of the river Gade at Two-waters; - thence through Kings Langley it passes through the parks of the Lords Clarendon and Essex till it meets the Colne valley above Rickmansworth.

From that junction it continues a varied course some lengths of it in Mill Streams and other parts out of them into and through the middle one of the three Mill Dams at Uxbridge.

From this chief point and level of water it takes a course of a new kind totally separate in respect of any Mill-rivers for it is restrained to that effect (or ought to be so) by a strong clause in the Act of Parliament.

From the said point it preserves its separate line six miles to a point of separation near Bull's Bridge over Craneford [sic] brook; having one branch fourteen miles long dead level cross the Brent and Kilburne [sic] valleys to the village of Paddington … and another branch six miles long passing to and down the Brent valley to the Thames at Brentford Bridge.

I have had occasion to be well acquainted with many portions of these rivers during thirty-five years on the subject of disputes at law or otherwise when the interests of one stream had ... to contend against the opposite; and on a variety of projects and speculations, which (fortunately for the Publick as well as individuals) were found in time to be visionary and elusive.

Another project for a canal previous to, and more inconsiderate even than this was schemed to pass the hills at Wendover, down the Missenden valley, from a summit level 474 feet above Thames level at Twickenham

Of the canal itself it has been examined from Brentford to and beyond the summit-level at Tring together with the short level branch ... to Paddington. It is necessary to state the general result of the Inspection, namely that, with a few exceptions, these two portions of the undertaking have been so erroneously and parsimoniously executed it is extremely subject to failure in the evil hour of a concurrence of circumstances ... in so much the Company (who [sic] have risked their capital in establishing it) have it not in their power *[to alter]* the relationship which they stand engaged in with you: that is to pay to furnish in a prompt and steady manner these waters which they have or may abstract without limitation from your possessions. ... It is true that the Act gives a power to use a certain portion of these waters ... from the summit at Uxbridge and **no farther**.

[In spite of temporary locks to cross the Ouse at Wolverton and a tramroad over Blisworth Hill, the Grand Junction Canal from Braunston to Brentford became a through route in October 1800. In August that year trials were carried out for boat passage over the Tring summit. It appears that Mylne attended these trials and reported accordingly.]

The water at the summit-level at Tring gradually failed from mid-August and that section was shut at the end of the month ... you therefore must be ruined by becoming a secondary interest when the number of boats, the soakage into the soil, the waste at the *[lock]* gates etc shall accrue so largely ... and be so frequent, your Mills etc. have no time to catch a share however small. If a lockful is brought from the summit it is called their own and is carried off as their legal property.

I found the whole of the summit-level ... and the navigable feeder from Wendover ... perfectly dry and empty on October 23rd.

MEANS OF SUPPLY

1. Springs under Tring Church-yard into Wendover feeder - shut down a week before my view.
2. Bulbourne Spring - dry.
3. Wendover reservoir - no good.

From all this it appears that this Wendover cutt [sic] became a consumer by absorption and evaporation instead of a feeder and surely in such arid soil, must ever continue so.

Now these are all and the only means of feeding the summit-level which exist, and I trust are correctly stated.

[Mylne was proved right. (See The Grand Junction Canal. A.H. Faulkner. 1972. David and Charles. Chapter 3. Tring and Braunston Summits.) He then deals with water demand under the headings of 1. Lockage. 2 Evaporation. 3. Leakage. and continues]

From thence - the ideal surface of water existing within these hills had sunk 20 feet or more perhaps, below that level which is necessary for trade in the summit-level. It is fair also to infer that, even that temporary and stationary lower level if it was worked off by the lockage of business, the suppositions surface that it might sink still lower. From whence, therefore, is the water to come which is to serve this summit-level.? All has been done which was thought necessary by their professional advisers, as appears, by the canal having been solemnly opened as a finished work for publick use.

How vain and visionary it has proved! ...The whole of these hills are in substance the most dry, broken, rotten stone and other calcarious [sic] matter which are to be found in this island; and the example of Sapperton Tunnel on a distant part of these hills might have afforded a precedent for well founded suspicion instead of unwary confidence.

ADDITIONAL WORKS PROPOSED

But let us see ... By a paper (apparently official) which has lately been handed to you; you are told there are for this case, other and sufficient resources ... without saying or attempting to account for why the same talents and principles ... have compleatly [sic] failed.

[This is a clear condemnation of Jessop followed up later. Mylne turns to reservoirs which he considered poor substitutes for adequate feeders. The Canal Company had reason to agree with him, for over the forty years after the line opened, no less than six reservoirs had to be constructed to serve the Tring summit with constant back pumping.]

They *[the reservoirs]* are of very modern application to such works and purposes as this canal ... First inventions, or the first application of old ones, are always held in undue and sanguine estimation ... as is mingling the headwaters from the other side.

[Mylne then reported at length on the canal "from Tring downwards". Some excerpts will suffice.]

Below Two-waters *[has occurred]* a compleat [sic] stoppage by a flap-door *[i.e. paddle]* being lifted up and jammed by a large boat sunk on the upper side to prevent it being opened.

[Application was made to the Civil Magistrates who declined to interfere.]

The cause was given out to be Lord Clarendon's cast iron bridge tumbling down and being rebuilt. Now that work was a long way below and the founds of the second bridge were laid by coffer dams long before without stopping the river at all. In work so publick, it is foolish to pretend to secrecy and the fatality, attending falsehood, might deter even the desperate … .

To proceed downwards, the canal line enters Badger Mill stream contrary to the original Act. Possession was taken of all the waters of the Colne as well as the Gade at this place where they are united. By means of the bed of the river Colne, the only reservoir of water … provided for the whole length between Tring and Brentford, is introduced at this level 242 feet below the summit and 153 feet above Brentford.

[Further on] At the lock on the canal opposite Moor-Park *[Lot Mead Lock]* … a fatal mistake was made in laying the sill of the lower gates so high in respect of the fixed and ancient level of the water at the junction of the Gade and Colne rivers that it became necessary on their part to raise the tumbling bays and overfalls established for time immemorial … a loaded barge could not get into the lock. The meadows of Mr Williams and many others as well as their Pleasure Gardens must continue to be under water.

[The canal passed over and obscured] Gutch-well to hide the deceit … I remember it well in its former state; I have of late had occasion to mark the sly pleasantry of their agents on this subject when mentioned by them with no small degree of self-complaisance … I left the subject to their exaltation and mention it now in this day of counting for retribution … the produce of this spring alone was ascertained in 1723 by Mr Jones and Mr C. Robinson to be 900 tons per hour … . This water belongs to the Mills below Uxbridge.

[After further detailed observations on the canal downwards Mylne continues]

I am now to request your attention to another part of your case in another part of the country. By the paper which was transmitted to you, information is given through the medium of Mr Barnes, the Resident and executing Engineer to this canal.

"That thirdly a reservoir may be made upon Riselip [sic] Common to extend over 120 acres of ground the whole contents of which may be given to the Millers in lieu of water to be taken from the Colne for the supply of the water-works of the Company."

I must say the Canal Company will be easily satisfied if, by the transmission of this paper, they take it for granted it will satisfy you also. … The reservoir will be of no use if ever executed. … The Engineers of this scheme (for as yet it is nothing else) don't seem to have ever studied the various divisions and interests of the Colne from Uxbridge downwards.

[Mylne declared that mention of water-works was a bluff to make everyone think that water was so ample that there was an intention to supply the needs or some needs of the "Metropolis". He refers to a resolution passed by the Grand Junction Canal Company's General Committee on 2nd June 1801]

"Resolved that the General Committee be directed forthwith to carry into execution the powers given them by law for better supplying this Metropolis with water" *[and comments]* If there is anywise foundation for such a thing being voted it must be as a truism.

When the long account of what is due to you, in all seasons and under all circumstances not yet combined, and the canal as yet untried, shall be satisfied by a due length of experience. … It would appear however that there is, with this Canal Company, some sort of ideal certainty of a right in your waters, or the waters of your rivers, streams etc.

[Moving towards conclusion Mylne refers to a report by Jessop dated Oct. 24th 1792, when the canal was proposed, in which Jessop mentions the expected water supply based "on Mr Barnes' measurements".]

On this superficial means, this project of 1792 has been realised in form but in respect of water it has not an existence in 1802. New Mill (near Tring) has been purchased, and its whole waters … swallowed up, to no effect. There is no other above the summit but Mr Hoare's in Wendover. That has not been purchased. … Where are the lower levels to be supplied, by this opinion, but by taking your streams: and for that reason, they were not mentioned; that it might not be known where the evil was to fall. You have felt it now with a witness.

By these opinions a reservoir is despaired of above Tring summit. … It is now sufficiently evident that the only two reservoirs provided for this canal are both below the summit at Tring. The waters in the soil are those only to be depended upon; and these failing in the middle of August, the loss of one foot in height put a compleat [sic] stop to all business in that quarter.

The remaining water in the summit was given to the Bucks Mills (Buckland); and the whole being empty they then only bethought themselves of repairing the works.

I have annexed a map of all the streams below Drayton that you may see the importance of the Question, as to your valuable establishments in that part of the Country … and I have added a plan of the canal that the object of this paper may be better understood.

I am with much respect
Your obedient Servant

Robert Mylne.

Appendix ii

Extracts from Robert Mylne's Journals 1793-1804.

Mylne's Business Journals from 1762 to 1810 have survived. They were in diary format, one week on the left hand page with an account sheet to the right. He noted receipts and disbursements meticulously on the account sheet and also expenses and fees to be charged against relevant daily entries but omitted pound signs if the figure quoted was in guineas. The excerpts quoted have been confined to the subject of this book with a few pertinent additions. The spelling of names is erratic, and the term 'dining' referred to the mid-day meal. Account entries are in brackets.

1793

JANUARY

24	Set off for Gloucester at Oxford.
25	At Gloucester.
26	At Stroud River and Whitminster - at Gloucester.
27	At Berkeley and the Severn.
28	At Gloucester.
29	At Newent and returned - chaise etc. to stand in lieu of maps bought for Gloucester navigation. Made a report to a committee viva-voce - long and minute - 5 guineas. At Gloucester.
30	Set off for London. - Bills at Gloucester and Berkeley being paid by Mr Comeline. £15-7-0 expenses.

FEBRUARY

18-20	Gave an estimate of the Gloucester and Berkeley in a new method altered from the former - 1. Attended a Committee on the Petition for the Gloucester and Berkeley Canal and gave evidence. Sent Mr Welles long report and estimate for the Gloucester and Berkeley and the 3 plans to be annexed thereto. (See 29 Jan.) Plans 15 + 5 = 20.
26	Attended 2nd reading of the Gloucester Canal Bill in H of C = 2.
28	Met Mr Welles on the Gloucester Canal.

MARCH

5	Attended the Gloucester - going to Mr Welles, Cecil Street, thence to Mr Webb's, Mortimer Street - gave explanations on various parts of the Canal - 2.
7	Attended Committee on Gloucester Canal settling the clauses etc. - went through the Bill - 3.
22	Attended at H of L. on Gloucester Canal - sworn-consultation - 3.
25	Attended Committee of Lords on Gloucester Canal. - Gave evidence - Bill gone through - 3.
28	Dined with the Gloucester Canal Committee. - Instructions given thereon.

SEPTEMBER

14	Left London for Gloucester. (Water at Maidenhead bridge 18" below springing course of arches) At Gloucester.
15/16	At Gloucester.
18	Attended a Committee, made report.
19	Went to Whitminster - finished at this place and moved onto Berkeley.
20	All day setting out Canal etc. at Berkeley. (Expenses by G and B canal - £12-10-2)
21	Left Berkeley - measured the Cam - Returned to Gloucester. Took levels and sounded the river.
22	Set off for Bristol with Mr Hall.
23	At the Cross Hands - Bath Road.
24	At Cirencester.
25	Rode out 6 hours on survey of line and waters - met several gentlemen but no report made.
26	At Gloucester.
27	Dined with Mr Comeline.
28	Dined with the Bristol Canal.
29	Dined with Mr Fendall.
30	Dined with the Berkeley. *[Committee]*

OCTOBER

1   Left Gloucester with Mr Small. (Disbursements to be paid by the proposed Canal from Bristol to Cirencester - £9-16-6. From Committee of Gloucester and Berkeley Canal. - £84-4-6 From Mr Watley for the subscriber to Gloucester and Berkeley Canal. - £30-0-0 Expenses by Gloucester and Berkeley Committee. - £13-12-2.)

1794

JANUARY

5   Then waited on Mr Cambridge on his mills and lands for Gloucester Canal and various parts of his works - long and tedious - 3.

8   Met Mr Fendall at Home - long explanations and descriptions of drawings of Gloucester Canal - 3.

11   Wrote long letter to Mr Fendall on Gloucester Canal business - 1.

15   All day at work on Gloucester Canal Estimates. (Expenses by Gloucester Canal. - £1-8-6.)

FEBRUARY

8   Wrote to Gloucester on canal **estimates.** Bricks.

22   Wrote to the Gloucester and Berkeley Canal a long letter on fire engines - P. earth *[Pozzolana?]*

MARCH

19   Gave Mr Triart [?] drawing of a digging engine for Gloucester and Berkeley Canal - to get a model thereof. - Long letter on fire engines.

21   Wrote to Gloucester and Berkeley Canal.

JUNE

5   Left town to go to Gloucester. - at Henley.

6   Went to Abingdon - at Brimscomb Port, House of the Company *[Thames and Severn]*.

7   Went down the Stroud canal to Whitminster - at Gloucester - began view.

8   Attended an irregular meeting - ditto - delivered drawings.

9   Attended a meeting of Committee all the forenoon and the whole day - dined together - went and examined Mr Trye's machine.

10   Set out the figure of the new bason [sic]. - the island, streets etc.

11   Set off for Berkeley - went to Branwood - Sharpness - Pillmouth - at Berkeley.

12   Went to S. side of Pill mouth and down to Merrett's house. - examined collateral cut - at Berkeley.

13   Committee at breakfast - went to Pillmouth - line of canal and colateral [sic] cut - went to Whitminster with Committee - at Gloucester.

14   All day setting out the bason and wharf - attended a meeting of the Committee.

15   Wrote 2 reports on the canal etc. and dined with Mr Fendall.

16   Attended Committee - made 2 long reports.

17   Dined with Committee - left Gloucester - at Burford.

18   At Oxford (From Committee of Gloucester and Berkeley Canal - bill of money paid for them - £44-5-0: 7/- for canvas to map of Gloucester and Berkeley Canal). (To Mr Smart - bill of models for Gloucester and Berkeley Canal - £12-15-6.)

AUGUST

7   Set out for Gloucester at one.

8   At Gloucester - conference with Mr Grazebrook until night.

9   Renewed conference with Mr Grazebrook - dined together.- Attended meeting of Committee - long conference between them and Mr Grazebrook on Bristol Canal.

10   Attended a Committee.

12   Attended a Committee and conference with Mr Grazebrook.

13   Set out for London at 5 by Cirencester - Burford and Oxford (Expenses by Gloucester and Berkeley received in a bill afterwards - £16-13-6.0)

SEPTEMBER

3   Wrote Mr Weaver a long letter on Gloucester Canal busines and sent Mr Wheeler - advert and 3 long particulars for digging the canal - the mason work and brickwork - very long and minute with form of proposals for each.

OCTOBER

18   Set off for Gloucester.

19	At Gloucester half past 4.
20	Dined at The Bell.
22	Dined with Mr Fendall - at Matson all night.
23	Called on by Mr Webb of the Lower George [?] to survey St. Nicholas Church and Steeple. - Dined with Mr Trye.
24	Surveyed and examined minutely the several parts of St. Nicholas Church and Steeple. - Dined at The Bell.
25	Dined with Dr. Cheston - a meeting.
26	Dined at The Sun.
27	Meeting at Gloucester - washed - dined with General Meeting - surveyed remainder of Business of St. Nicholas - at Ham *[Home?]*.
28	Attended Committee of Gloucester and Berkeley Canal - set off for London.
29	At Buscot Park

NOVEMBER

7	Wrote long report with drawing annexed on St. Nicholas Church and Steeple in G. Weston after repeated surveys, views and drawings - to the Bishop of Gloucester. - 10
	(From Committee of Gloucester and Berkeley a bill of money 5. Advanced from bank - £44-5-0. From Committee of Gloucester and Berkeley Navigation on account of Salary and applied as above - £150-0-0. To Messrs Hibbett's and Co. **10% on 10 shares** Gloucester and Berkeley Canal - £100-0-0. From Gloucester and Berkeley a bill of travel expenses - £70-3-10 and also salary up to September 1st 1794 - Expenses by Gloucester and Berkeley Canal - £15-9-9)
21	(Gloucester and Berkeley Canal for carriage of printed particulars - 2/8.)

1795

MARCH

	(To Mr Troughton - tape measures for Gloucester and Berkeley Canal 16/-.)
19	Set out for Gloucester - at Wickham.
20	At Gloucester at 7.
22	Dined with Mr Fendall at Matson.
23	Breakfast with Mr Weaver.
25	Dined with Mr Chandler.
26	Dined with Dr. Lysons at Gloucester.
29	Dined with Mr Comeline.

APRIL

1	Left Gloucester.

MAY

16	To Gloucester.
18	Meeting of Committee advertised - dined at Boothall.
20	Dined at Boothall.
21	Leave of absence, dined with Mr Fendall at Matson.
22	Came to town.
24	Dined with Mr Saunders.
26	Committee - dined at Mr Raikes - at Matson.
27	In Gloucester.
28	Left The Bell.
29	Committee.
31	Dined with Dr. Cheston.

JUNE

1	Set off for London at half past 5. At Burford.
	(From Gloucester and Berkeley arrears of salary to Xmas - 1794 £200-0-0: From ditto bill of travelling expenses - £73-3-10. From Gloucester and Berkeley half years Salary - £175-0-0.)

JULY

2	Set off for Gloucester at 2 - at Tetsworth.
3	Committee attended.
4	At Gloucester.
5	Went to Mr Fendalls at Matson.
7	Attended Committee - 6.
8	Set off for London.

Appendix ii

AUGUST
20   Set off for Gloucester at 2 - at Tetsworth at 9.
21   At Gloucester at 4 - a meeting.
22   A meeting.
24   A Committee - some business done - no quorum - at Matson.
25   A Committee - no meeting - set off for London.
        (Expenses by Gloucester and Berkeley £18-7-7: Deduct for expenses of 2 daughters £2-7-7: From Mr Webb for report on Survey of St. Nicholas Church £10-0-0: Expenses by Gloucester and Berkeley £16-15-3: To Mr Norton in part model of bridges for Gloucester and Berkeley £3-3-0. ditto in full £1-1-0: From Gloucester and Berkeley half salary - £175-0-0)

SEPTEMBER
18   Mr Dadford came to Gloucester.
28   Meeting at Gloucester - adjourned a fortnight.

OCTOBER
3   Left town at 2.
6   At Gloucester at 12 - viewed works - attended Committee Meeting.
7   Committee meeting at 12.
8   Absent
10   Old Minas day[?] - surrender of dun's etc. [sic]
11   At Matson - ditto.
12   General Meeting.
13   At Matson - Left Gloucester at 6.

DECEMBER
28   To Gloucester at 10.
29   At Gloucester half past 3.
30   Attended meeting of Committee.
31   Dined at Matson - all night there.
        (Expenses by Gloucester and Berkeley - £15-0-0: To Mr Troughton for Gloucester and Berkeley Canal - £4-4-0: Expenses by Gloucester and Berkeley £7-10-6.)

1796
        (From Gloucester and Berkeley Canal Co. - £17-10-0. Money advanced to Mr Troughton - £4-4-0 and Mr Norton - £13-6-0)

JANUARY
1   At Matson. Attended Committee. - Mr Comeline and Dadford dined with me - at Gloucester.
2   Went on line beyond Hempsted Hill to Dr. Lysons for a house - Elsmore Land - setting out the middle line - Mr Dadford dined with me.
3   Mr Thomas, Mr Pinkerton and Mr Pixston did business with them for the Company all forenoon - dined with Mr Comeline.
4   Attended a Committee.
5   Went along the Canal and set out central line as far as half a mile beyond and South of Russers Lane - dined at home - Mr Dadford at night.
6   Attended Committee - dined at home - supp'd at home
8   General Meeting and Supp't there.
9   Dined at Mr Weavers, Committee in evening - supp't at home with Mr Dadford.
10   Set off for London with Mr Mills [?] in his chaise to Frog Mill - at Oxford.
        (Expenses by Gloucester and Berkeley - £6-11-0)

MARCH
24   Set off for Gloucester half past 1 - at Oxford at 10.
25   A early off at half past 6 - At Gloucester at 2.
26   Committee held.
27   Easter Sunday - went to Matson - all night.
28   General Meeting at Gloucester - attended all day - dined.
29   A Committee held.
30   Set out lines of Bason.

APRIL
1   Committee held.

2	Set out New Bridge and its roads. - Set out Hempsted Avenue etc. - Sounded the river - dined with Mr Mee.
3	Attended Mr Whitworth at office - explained the plan and the execution - surveyed line to Hardwicke Court - dined Kingshead with Whitworth and Dadford.
4	Committee held. - LAID THE FIRST STONE.
5	Set off at 6 - at Cirencester.
6	Set off at 6 - in town by half past 7.

MAY

12	To Gloucester set of half past 2 - Mr Jessop in company. Slept at Tetsworth.
13	At Gloucester at half past 4. - Went and viewed Bason etc. and line of canal to Hempsted and half a mile further.
	(From Messrs Fendal and Co. Gloucester - £70-0-0. ditto - £100-0-0. Horse hire and Dadsford tools to London. 13/-. From Gloucester and Berkeley Canal. Salary - £175-0)
14	Examined plans at office - set off on view along line to Lord Hardwicke's to Pegthorne Hill, Stroud Mill, Stroud Canal, Whitminster, new line - to Frampton - luncheon - to Saul's Worth - to Cambridge Brook - to Berkeley - to Newport - stop't.
15	Went to line at Berkeley - along it to Bason, Pill-mouth etc. - returned to colateral cut - luncheon - along line whole way to Cambridge Brook. - Returned to Gloucester.
16	Consultation with **Mr Jessop** - attended meeting of Committee. **Mr Jessop** made report viva voce - dined with Committee.
17	**Mr Jessop** went off to Birmingham and home. Dined at home.
18	Dined at home.
19	Dined at home.
20	Attended Committee - Received letters and plan from Portsmouth - wrote letters on that harbour to **Jessop** - Huddart, Knight, Greetham on that subject.
21	Went along the canal line, set out well for engine near the stone bench *[Lower Rea?]* - went cross over to Matson.
22	Finished estimates - surveyed house at Creed Place - dined at Matson.
23	Walked and breakfasted at Gloucester.
24	Bored 24ft below bason - dined with Mr Howard - Left Gloucester - at Frog Mill.

AUGUST

11	Left town for Gloucester at 2.
12	At Gloucester at 3. Attended meeting of Committee.
13	Went a survey of the works in hand.
15	At General Meeting - vote on me 205 against: 252 for.
17	Mr Yenn's dinner. *[Smeatonian Society]*
18	Leave of absence.
19	Dined with Mr Greenaway.
20	Set off - went to Duke of Norfolk's in Herefordshire - returned
	(Gloucester and Berkeley share 10% - £140-0-0. Gave Mr Jelfe a draft on Gosling to put my cash into a balance nearby - £55-0-0: Journey to Duke of Norfolk's, expenses to and return halved with Mr Green[away] - £1-8-0: Bill at Kings Head - £3-7-4. Expenses by Gloucester and Berkeley Canal £19-17-6).
22	A Committee - dined in Company.
23	Set off at 6 - at Frog Mill.

SEPTEMBER

22	Set off for Gloucester at half past 2.
23	At Gloucester at half past 2 - A Committee held at 7 - dined with Corporation - no supper.
25	Dined at Cam[bridge] - no supper.
26	General Meeting at Gloucester - dined at Boothall - no supper.
27	4 [to] Breakfast - dined at Matson, slept there.
28	Dined at Jelfe[s].
29	Break - dined at Saunders.

OCTOBER

1	Dined at Jelfe[s] - Committee
2	Went along line to far end of works, then Standish Park - dined at Matson - slept there.
3	Break.
4	Set off at 6 - at Frog Mill.

DECEMBER

26	Set off for Gloucester at 10. At Witney at half past 7.

27	At Gloucester at 2. - tried a Committee - none.
28	Dined with Jelfe - supper at home.
29	Dined at home.
30	Dined at home.
31	Settled Proposals for Messrs Sharpe and Tayler.

(To Mr Faden for Gloucester and Berkeley Canal Co. - £1-5-6. From Mr Wheeler - 2 bills to be paid Mr Troughton and Faden - £2-3-6. Expenses by Gloucester and Berkeley Canal - £17-14-11; From Gloucester and Berkeley Canal Co. half salary - £175-0-0. To Mr Fendall on his Atlas 10/6 - Mr Comeline - proxy 7/-: To Mr Dadford - horse hire 14/-.)

1797

JANUARY

1	At Gloucester - dined and walked at Matson - stayed all night.
2	Returned to Gloucester - a Committee held all forenoon to settle bill of variation - dined at Kings Head with Committee.
3	A Committee at office on the Bill - settled contract with Messrs Stroud and Cook[e].
4	Settled explanation of contract with Messrs Stroud and Cook[e] - dined at home.
5	Went the survey of whole line as far as Hardwicke Court - dined at home - Dadford with me - supper. Dadford and Stroud.
6	Committee held - dined at home - £15-0-0 from bankers.
7	Dined with Mr Comeline.
8	Dined with Mr Saunders.
9	Mr Comeline dined with me.
10	A Committee held - set off for town at 4.

FEBRUARY

24	Attended and gave evidence on Petition of Gloucester and Berkeley Canal at House of Commons.
25	Went with Messrs Welles and Comeline to Mr Cambridge at Richmond for his assent etc.

(To Mr Dadford - horse hire 14/-. By Gloucester and Berkeley Canal £18-0-0. From Gloucester and Berkeley Canal Co. Travel expenses - £92-1-0.)

MARCH

28	Attended Committee of Commons on new bill for Gloucester and Berkeley Canal - when it passed. - Furnished plans, estimates etc.

APRIL

27	Sworn at House of Lords - Gloucester and Berkeley Canal Bill.

MAY

1	House of Lords - Gloucester and Berkeley Canal bill - passed.
11	Set out for Gloucester at 2. - At Tetsworth at half past 8.
12	At Gloucester half past 3 - a Committee.
14	Breakfast - Mr Dadford went with me along whole line - examined fire engine - Mr Dadford dined with with me - no supper.
15	Alone - dined at home.
17	Went to Whitminster - set out crossing etc. made views - went to Frampton Pill - considered access to Slimbridgeworth - mouth of Pill - dined at Frampton Green - carried Mr Bayliss - returned to Gloucester.
21	Went along the line.
22	General Meeting - attended.
23	A Committee.
25	Went a survey - Frampton Green - Framilode, Epray, Whitminster, Frampton Pill.
26	A Committee - dined with Comeline. Another Committee.
27	Set out quarter past 6 - at Frogmill at half past 8.

(Kings Head-Servants - £7-12-0. Spent for Gloucester and Berkeley Canal Co. - £17-0-0)

28	Off at half past 5 - In London half past 8.

AUGUST

9	Assizes at Gloucester.

(FromGloucester and Berkeley Canal half years salary to Mich. last when the same was ceased by agreement and changed to - £4-4-0 per diem (See Sept 23 to come) - £175-0-0; Expenses Gloucester and Berkeley Canal - £1-12-0: Spent for Gloucester and Berkeley Canal Co. - £20-14-0)

SEPTEMBER

21	Set out for Gloucester at quarter past 2.
22	At Gloucester half past 4. No Committee as expected.
23	A Committee held totally on my salary - committed it into an allowance of 4 gns per diem.
24	Dined at Matson - all night.
25	Breakfast with Jelfe. A Committee - a general meeting.
26	Breakfast with Jelfe - went along line on foot to Hempsted Bridge - home.
27	Home.
28	Went on horseback along line.
30	Sir G. Paul all forenoon.

OCTOBER

1	Home - Mr Weaver on Mr Dadford - Matson - home.
2	Sir G. Paul all forenoon - Mayors feast - Dadford broke out - home.
3	Home - A Committee held.- Mr Comeline's - not home - apology and pardon by Dadford.
4	Home - At Fendalls.
5	At home.
6	Home - A Committee held.
7	Set off to Berkeley - there by half past 3. Viewed Berkeley Pill again - at Berkeley.
8	Rode to Purton Pasage - walked to Kingston Pill - rode back - then walked to Sharpness Point and rode home - at Berkeley.
9	Set off and walked 1 and a half miles to Newport. At Bath by half past 2.

1798

FEBRUARY

24	Emila died in the morning at Southampton.

MARCH

7	Robert set off from Brest.
13	Received a letter from Robert in France *[as a Prisoner of War.]*
19	Sent to Mr Wheeler - Gloucester, a letter in answer on the new wharf wall which has failed - 2.

APRIL

9	Wrote Mr Wheeler and sent him a long section of Canal.
18	Robert will get to Melun.
	(Messrs Niblet Evans and Co. Gloucester - money to be lodged there on my account. - £41-0-0.)

JULY

20	Gloucester and Berkeley Canal. Wrote a long letter to Mr Wheeler on a law suit about Pinkerton's Contract. (Sent Robert by post to Dover. £7-0-0.)

NOVEMBER

17	Robert set off for Portsmouth and Gibraltar with £25-0-0 in pocket and £40-0-0 in agents hands. - embarked aboard the "Minerva" - Capt. Crokbank [sic].

DECEMBER

8	Robert died at sea aboard the "Minerva" Frigate on passage to Gibraltar.
	(To Messrs Ross and Ogilvie for Robert to buy Lieut's Commisssion £150-0-0.) *[This was never completed and the draft returned.]*

1799

JANUARY

25	The news of Robert's death.

SEPTEMBER

30	General meeting at Gloucester.

1800

MARCH

24   (To Mr Wheeler for a sum erroneously received by Mr Jelfe and 5 years quarter interest thereof to Lady Day 1800 - to pay postage. £9-0-0.)

JULY

(Paid into Messrs Robarts, Curtis and Co for Messrs Fendal [sic] and Co. Gloucester, for Gloucester and Berkeley Canal draft - £84-12-8.)

NOVEMBER

13   Conversed with Mr Williams on his business at Rickmansworth.

15   Held a correspondence of 5 letters on my part with **Mr Jessop** about a view etc. at Rickmansworth.

16   Held a long conference with **Mr Jessop** on the matters in dispute at Rickmansworth between the Navigation there and Mr Williams on Mills, gauge Waters etc.

20   Wrote 2 letters to Rickmansworth on the business there.

22   ditto on **Mr Jessop's** disappointing me.

23   Set out with **Mr Jessop** to Rickmansworth on the dispute between Messrs Williams, Earle and Salter on one part and the Grand Junction Canal Co. and Messrs Strutts' on the other - began at mills - viewed Millhead, tail, round wharfing below - requested head to be lowered - refused - then granted in part, but not done in all its parts - the water when lowered was stopt at sluices or opening - went then up to tumbling bay - then to trunk - then to lock - then to Weybeards water courses.

24   Water pent up to highest - went to Mr Earle's - then up to his meadows - down the Colne to Whitbridge [?] - then into his lower grounds - then down to weirs, lock, tumbling bay and mills - then into Pleasure Grounds - at cottage - examined witnesses, Mr Salter, Gardner and Swannard[1] - **Mr Jessop** went away and left me.

25   Writing particulars - making plans - examined drawings - documents - Mr Holland present. Examined Swannard - rained hard, could not go out.

26   Returned to London in Mr Williams' chaise - Edgware - another to New River Head.

30   Worked all day on the business at Rickmansworth; drawings, Minutes etc.

1801

MARCH

16   Went to House of Commons − examined the votes − found a petition of the Grand Junction Canal on the − dispute at Rickmansworth.

17   Wrote to Mr Swannell[1] on dispute.

26   Attended a meeting of delegates of Grand Junction Canal − on dispute − stated the whole matter − heard a proposition from them − agreed to see Mr Barnes on it by way of trial. Waited on Mr Barker[2] on all this.

APRIL

2   Called at Grand Junction Canal office − conference - Mr Gray[3] there − then again at House of Commons with him and Mr Barker on Mr Williams' business.

3   Wrote Mr Williams another letter on this business and the new Bill.

21   Mr Swannel[1] called on the business at Rickmansworth − 1 hour conversation.

22   Attended House of Commons on a Committee of the Grand Junction Canal and Mr Williams and Co. interest therein − presented my draft clause.

24   Not at Wapping [London Docks]/Sick. [Mylne was 68.]

29   Attended Committee of [House of]Commons on Mr Williams' business.

30   Called Swannel[1] and Aubrey [?] and gave notice.

AUGUST

8   7 days a week /work/not to be allowed after this − notice thereof given.

OCTOBER

10   Went on a survey of Grand Junction Canal − began at Paddington − went along canal to Greenford Green − left off there − crossed over to Brentford Cut near Brent Bridge - went down the canal to Brentford Bridge. Returned to London.

20   For Greenford Green − Uxbridge all night.

21   Rickmansworth and Watford all night.

22   At Tring all night.

23   At St. Albans.

24   At Amwell. [Mylne's country home.]

NOVEMBER

17   Went to a meeting at Hounslow of the Millers on the *[River]* Colne — made a long report viva voce on the Grand Junction Canal — its present state — the deficiency of water - the trade etc — very long, minute etc.

1802

JANUARY

25   Wrote Mr Loveden a long letter on Thames Navigation from Lechlade to Mapledurham.

FEBRUARY

10   Long consultation with Mr Millard *[resident surveyor]* on the upper districts of the Thames. The works proposed in 1791 *[by Jessop]* — the parts thereof not done and on three new propositions of improvements.

11   Report in writing — sent to Mr Loveden for a meeting at Oxford on three cuts proposed to be made in the 5 and 6 districts. Gave it to Mr Millard going to Oxford.

18   Meeting Thames Commissioners at Westminster.

23   Waited on the Duke of Northumberland — a long conversation on his dispute on the *[calico]* printing ground, waters etc — The Grand Junction Canal — the Millers question — the division of the river Colne near Drayton — 2 hrs.

MARCH

4   Duke of Northumberland *[on various disputes]* - gave also a copy of a drawing of the London Canal — to show his river in all its parts and connections and particulars added thereto.

13   Long discussion on the dispute with the Grand Junction Canal.

30   Met Committee of Millers — went to Drayton — set out the point of partition of both streams leading to the Duke's, the King's and Stanwell *[Hanwell?]* streams — many persons present — called witnesses.

APRIL

2   Waited on Duke of Northumberland — made report on Drayton Point.

15   Set out for Lechlade on a survey of the Thames but made a view of part of the Grand Junction Canal.

16   At Wendover — surveyed Hoare's Mills and cut to Tring — at Buscot House — Mr Loveden.

MAY

15   Went to Hounslow — meeting of Gentlemen Millers — made report on the whole business of the Grand Junction Canal — their complaints and the cause thereof — very long - many calculations — much matter.

JUNE

3   Gave Mr Loveden for the Commissioner of the 5th and 6th Districts a special report on 4 new Cuts proposed, long and particular with 4 drawings annexed thereto.

6   Mr Loveden dined with me — conversation on the Thames Navigation.

26   Went to a meeting of Millers at Hounslow - on complaints against the Grand Junction Canal — consultations — gave advice on measures to be pursued.

30   Wrote and sent Mr Clark a long part of a Mun: [?] to the Grand Junction Canal Co. under various heads of engineering.

JULY

30   Long conversation with Mr Lintal on behalf of Duke of Northumberland and Millers — relating to his duty on Grand Junction Canal.

AUGUST

14   Went to Duke of Northumberland's - gave him report on the Grand Junction Canal — 2. Examined place for a boat house and temple[4] over it — took dimensions of site and orders for a design — viewed the water etc.

OCTOBER

2   Went to Syon — gave 4 drawings, washed, for a Summer and Boat House.

26   Went to a meeting of Millers at Hounslow — on complaints against the Grand J.

Appendix ii

NOVEMBER

23   Wrote long letter to Duke of Northumberland - on the business of his river - on the Grand
          Junction Canal — and sent him a long paper of instructions for his river Surveyor.

DECEMBER

6   Waited on Messrs Brogdan and Paine — 2 or 3 times at the House of Commons on the
          Duke of Northumberland's business — could not find them.

11   Waited on Mr Paine and Mr Sterling for Duke of Northumberland on the new Bill of the
          Grand Junction Canal on a remedy for the old one — long consultation.

1803

[*Boat House at Syon built. Mylne visited five times.*]

DECEMBER

27   Read over, considered and took minutes of a Bill in Chancery to be filed against Grand
          Junction Canal by the Millers etc on the Colne — 52 sheets.

1804

JANUARY

7   All day at work on a bill to be filed against Grand Junction Canal Co. — altering,
          correcting the draft thereof made by Mr Stanley.

NOTES

1.   Variously Swannale , Swannell or Swannard.
2.   John Barker, Surveyor, assistant to Barnes.
3.   Edward Oakley Gray. Solicitor and Clerk to the Company.
4.   Still attributed to James Wyatt.

Appendix iii

Waterways with which Robert Mylne was involved in one capacity or another.

Year	Works	Note
1760-1769	Thames at Blackfriars.	
1767-1810	New River Co.	
1768	Limehouse Canal - London.	
1768	Dingley Cut - River Lee.	
1769	Grand Western Canal.	2
1770	Leeds and Liverpool Canal.	
1789	Cromford Canal.	1
1790	Staffordshire and Worcester.	
1790	Leeds and Liverpool Canal.	2
1790	Severn Navigation.	1
1790	Stourport Cut.	
1790	Thames and Severn Canal.	1,2
1791	Eau Brink Cut.	1
1791-1802	Thames Navigation.	1
1792	Trent Navigation.	1
1792	Erewash Navigation.	
1792	Nottingham Canal.	1
1792	Rochdale Canal.	1,3
1792	Ouze Drainage Navigation.	1,3
1792	Oxford Canal.	
1792	Braunston and Hampton Gay Canal.	1,3
1792	Grantham Group	
	- Witham, Mowbush and Esdale Canals.	1
1792	River Don, Stainforth Cut and Thorne Canal.	
1792	Dove and Dearn Navigation.	
1792	Barnsley Canal.	1
1792	Sheffield and Eckington Canal	3
1792	Lancaster Canal (North branch)	1,3
1792	Grand Junction Canal.	1
1793	Bristol and Cirencester Canal.	
1793	Gloucester and Berkeley Canal.	1,2
1793	Trent Navigation.	1,3
1793	Great Western Canal.	1,3
1793	Exeter and Taunton Navigation.	1
1793	Somerset Canal.	1
1793	Crediton Canal.	
1793-1794	London (Taplow to Isleworth) Canal.	2
1793	Kennet and Avon Canal.	3
1796	Chelmer Navigation.	
1796	Medway Navigation.	1
1797	Somerset Coal Canal.	1
1800-1801	Grand Junction Canal.	1
1804	Portsmouth Canal.	
1804	Grand Surrey Canal (Croydon).	1

Note
with:
1.   *William Jessop.*
2.   *Robert Whitworth.*
3.   *John Rennie the elder.*

Appendix iv

List of Engineering Works transcribed from the Journals of Robert Mylne.

1760	Committee	Blackfriars Bridge
1763	Mr Preston	Stockton Bridge
1764	Sir Edward Deering	Cowley Bridge
	Mr Heard	Work on Westbury Level - Barking
1765	Duke of Portland	Bridge at Welbeck
	Earl of Warwick	Bridge at Warwick
1766	Mr Powel	Uxbridge River Report.
	Dr Adams	Shrewsbury Bridge
	Mr Symons	Advice on Port of Bristol
1767	New River Co	Westham Waterworks - River Lee
	New River Co	New River
	Duke of Atholl	River works at Atholl
	Commissioners of Customs	Haven and Wet Dock Hull
	Apothecarys' Company	Embankment on River Thames
1768	Mr Lockwood	Layout of Cut to Limehouse
	River Lee Trustees	Mr Dingley's Cut
	Capt. Digby	Bridge
	Lord Ilchester	Bridge
	Mrs Talbot	Bridge at Uxbridge
	Duke of Argyll	Repairs Dumbarton Bridge
1769	Mr Mytton	Woodbridge, Halston
	Bishop of Londonderry	Bridge
1770	Mr Denison	Chelsea Garden Wharf
	Mr Baynes	New yard and wharf
1771	Mr Michel	Opinion on River Thames and Survey
	Mr Frame	Repairs to Bridge at Chelmsford
1772	Bishop of Durham	Rebuilding Newcastle Bridge
	Bishop of Durham	Bridge repairs at Durham
	Lord Abingdon	Swynford Bridge
	Duke of Argyll	Bridges at Inveraray
	Glasgow Corporation	Bridge at Glasgow
1773	Sir Abraham Hume	Bridge at Wormleybury
	Kent County	Tonbridge Bridge
1774	Mr Taylor	Report on Warwick Bridge
	Mr Greenway	Report on Warwick Bridge
	Mr Hill	Bridge at Tern
	Mr Parker	Bridge at Cobham
	Mr Parker	Bridge at Leatherhead
	Mr Woodhouse	Footbridge
	Surrey County (?)	Removing Mitcham Bridge
1775	Sir George Colebrooke	Rebuilding Reigate Bridge
	Yarmouth Corporartion	Report on haven, pier and wharf
		North Elmham Bridge
	Mr Mill	Bridge over small stream
1777	Mr Owen	Bridge at Brunhyn
	Commissioners of Sewers	Report on New Cut, banks and river at Stonar-Sandwich and bridges.
1778	Mr Mytton	Bridge on ropes. Halston
1780	Dr Cust	Report and alterations Wells Harbour
1782	Hants County	Romsey Bridge
1783	Mr Fenwick	Dam at Bywell on Tyne
	Hexham Corporation	Hexham Bridge
	Hants County	Ilford Bridge
1784	Mr Sloane	Facade of South Stoneham Bridge
1785	Northumberland County	Chollerford Bridge
	Northumberland County	Ridley Hall Bridge
1786	Irish Society	Bridge at Londonderry
	Mr Slade	Bridge at Boston
	Mr Smith	Dam and Pond at Putney Hill
1787	Commissioners of Customs	Report on Dungeness

	Mr Agassiz	Margate Harbour and Pier (Lighthouse)
	Mr Sawkins	Report on Portsmouth Docks
	Mr Sawkins	Report on Gosport Fortifications
	Mr Sawkins	Brewery and Cooperage, Gosport
	Corporatation	Ilchester Bridge
1788	Lord Macdonald	Report on Hebrides Fisheries
1789	Mr Patterson	Report on Mills and Waterworks, Norwich
	Committee of City Lands	Wharf at Puddle Dock
	Duke of Northumberland	Report on River Colne
	Mr Graham	Cromford Canal
	Mr Strutt	Colne Mills, Report
	Magistrates of Edinburgh	Report on City Water Supply
	Earl Breadalbane	Bridges at Taymouth
	Corporation (?)	Derby Waterworks and Mills
1790	Mr Black	Worcester and Staffordshire Canal
	Mr Longbottom	Liverpool and Leeds Canal
	Mr Young	Severn Navigation
	Mr Fieldhouse	An Engine to scour River Severn
	Mr Chambers	Thames and Severn Navigation
1791	Mr Ross	Montrose Bridge
	Mr Loveden	St John's Bridge at Buscot
	Thames Commissioners	Survey of Thames
	Sir George Rouse	Bridge and Causeway, Lowestoft
	Mr Golborne	Eau Brink Cut
	Kings Lynn Corporation	Waterworks and Harbour
	Mr Burden	Sunderland Bridge
1792	Mr Cradock	Erewash Navgation
	Mr Rennie	Rochdale Canal
	Duke of Newcastle	Opposition to Grantham Canal
	Sir Robert Sutton	River Devon Navigation (?Suffolk)
	Mr Black	Ten mile Canal - Oxon (?Hampton Gay)
	Leith Corporation	Harbour, Bridge, Pier, Docks etc.
	Duke of Northumberland	Braunston and Hampton Gay Canals
	Southampton Corporation	Quays, Piers and Docks
	Mr Dixon	Witham, Mowbush and Esdale Canals
	Mr Thompson	Don River, Stainforth Cut, Thorne Canal and Quay
	Committee	Dearne and Dove Canal
	Committee	Barnsley Canal
	Mr Crosley	Calder Navigation
	Committee	Sheffield and Eckington Canal
1793	Mr Welles	Gloucester and Berkeley Canal
	Mr Sparrow	Trent Navigation
	Sir George Young	Grand Western Canal
	Mr Gray	Crediton Canal
	Mr Crowther	London Canal
	City Commissioners	Survey of Fleet Ditch
1794	Town Corporation	Hull Docks and Harbour
	Mr Rollestone	Kennet and Avon Canal
	Duke of Bolton	Hackwood Waterworks
	Thames Commissioners	Survey of River Thames
	Navy Commissioners	Gosport Fort, Docks and Bridges
1795	Sir R. Holkam	Pier at Bognor
	Mr More	Aberdeen Harbour
1796	Sir Chales Saxton	Portsmouth Harbour
	Mr Tindal	Chelmsford Canal Arbitration
	Sir William Bishop	Maidstone Canal Arbitration
	Mr Hamerton	Hackney Waterworks
1797	Mr Hulme	Manchester Waterworks
	Mr Sloane	Northam Bridge, Itchin
	Mr Conant	Dunhearston Coal Canal
	Mr Cowper	Altering River, Tewin, Hertfordshire
1798	Corporation	Norwich Waterworks
	Corporation	Yarmouth Harbour
	Mr Burley	Bridge and Lake at Exton
	Earl Breadalbane	Taymouth Park Bridge

1799	Mr Dance	Limehouse Wharfs
	Mr Dance	Blackwall Docks
	Mr Williams	Opposition to Grand Junction Canal
1800	Port of London	Plan for London Bridge
	Mr Vaughan	London Docks
1801	Duke of Northumberland	Survey of Isleworth River
	Bridge Committee	Survey of London Bridge
	Mr Williams	Survey of Grand Junction Canal
1802	Mr Loveden	Survey of River Thames
	Mr Dance	Repairs to Rochester Bridge
	Port of London	Removal of Blackwall Rock
1803	Navy Commissioners	Water Supply, Plymouth Docks
1805	East India Company	Plan for Prince of Wales Island
1806	Vestry	Water Supply. Shoreditch Church
	Lord Bovingdon	Embankment, Catwater. Plymouth
1807	Mr Dallas	East London Water Works
	Navy Commissioners	Woolwich Docks
1808	Common Serjeant	Opposition to Savoy Bridge
1809	Mr Patteson	Bridge at Norwich
	Mr Nash	Vauxhall Bridge
	Mr Chamberlayne	Bridge at Thorpe
	Corporation(?)	Report on Dublin Water Works
1810	Mr Disney	Survey of part of the Gloucester and Berkeley Canal.

Appendix v

List Of Architectural Works transcribed from the journals of Robert Mylne

1762	Lord Morton	Bookroom at Chysick House in Brook Street and Stables
1763	Mr Douglas	St Cecilia's Hall, Edinburgh
	Mr Southwell (Lord de Clifford)	Kingsweston House
	Lord Garlies	House in Galloway
	Mr Webbs	House at Petersham
	Mr Patteson	House at North Elham, Norfolk
1764	Marquis of Lorne	Alterations to Argyll House
	Mr Mytton	Alterations to Halston
	Marquis of Lorne	House in Scotland
	Sir Edward Deering	House in London
	Mr Briscoe	Alterations at Twickenham
	Mr Briscoe	Alterations at Cheapside
	Lord Garlies	House in London
	Mr Almack	Club in St James
	Sir Wiliam Wiseman	House
	Mr Murray	House at Cally
	Mr Murray	Inn at Cally
	Sir William Duncan	2 Houses in London
	Lady Susan Stewart	Alterations
	Sir William Knatchbull	Design for Mersham
	Mr Hotchkiss	Malt Kiln
	Major Hamilton	House in London
1765	St Bartholomew's Hospital	Extension
	Mr Webster	House
	Society of Arts	6 Plans
	Sir Henry Manwaring	House
	Mr Southwell's Mother	House in London
	Mr Chambers	House at Totteridge
	Earl of Warwick	Alterations to Castle
	Mr Fermor	Tusmore House
	Mr Farr	Lodge House at Bristol
	Mr Woodfall	House in Green street
1766	Maquis of Lorne	Alterations to Marlborough Mews
	Sir Abraham Hume	Wormleybury
	Mr Strahan	House
	Miss Leighton	Alterations to Condover, Salop
	Dr Hunter	Alterations to House in Litchfield Street
	Mr De Salis	Work at Basildon
	Lord Eglintoune [sic]	Alterations
	Mr Charteris	Alterations to House and Castle at Haddington
	Earl of Lauderdale	Alterations at Hatton
	Mr Bishop	House at Islington
	Sir George Colebrook	Work at Gatton
	Sir Brook Bridges	Work at Goodneston
	Duke of Portland	House in London
1767	Dr Dechair	Chapel Roof in Bath
	Mr Wedderburn	Summerhouse in Scotland
	Mr Bindley	Alterations to House at Caversham
	Mr Prescot	Work at Theobald's Park
	Mr Murray	Repairs in Portman Square
	Lord Archibald Hamilton	Repairs in Portman Square
	Lord Garlies	Repairs to House in Charles Street
	Mr Fullerton	House
1768	Mr J. Mill	House in Scotland
	Mr Jeffries	Alterations at Hanwell
	Mr Brown	House at Peckham
	Sir Francis Gosling	House at Fulham

1769	Mr Hill	House at Tern
	Mr Harvey	House at Claybury
	Duke of Argyll	Alterations to Rosneath Castle
	Sir John Whitefoord	House in Edinburgh
	Mr Berners	Work at Hanwell
	Mrs Talbot	Work at Uxbridge
1770	Sir Harbord Harbord	House
	Mr Patteson	Lying-In Hospital, London
	Mr Allen	Infirmary at Belfast
	Archbishop of Canterbury	Repairs to Croydon Palace
	Mr I. Campbell	House at Edinburgh
	Mr Dennison	Layout of Estate, Apothecarys' Co.
	Treasurer	Layout of Estate, Bridewell Hospital
	Mr Durand	Woodcote House. extensions
	Mr Gosling	Whitton House
1771	Sir George Colebrooke	Church at Gatton
	Mr Mostyn	House in Montgomeryshire
1772	Mr Wedderburn	Drawings for Lincolns' Inn
	Mr Wedderburn	Plans for Old Playhouse, Portugal Street
	Mr Wedderburn	Plans for General Register Office
	Mr Trecothick	Addington House
	Bishop of Durham	Repairs to Durham Castle
	Mr Barrow	Altering House at Twickenham
	Lord Abingdon	Alterations at Rycot [*Radcot*]
	Lord Abingdon	Additions at Rycot
	Lord Abingdon	Additions at Whitham [*Wytham*]
	Lord Abingdon	Inn at Swynford Bridge
	Duke of Argyll	Work at Inveraray
	Lord Hamilton	Work at Hamilton Palace
	Bishop of Durham	Alterations Auckland House
1773	Mr Owen	House at Brunhyn
	Mr Owen	House at Woodhouse, Wales
	Miss Leighton	Loton Park, Salop
	Col. Skene	House at Pitlour, Fifeshire
	Lord Stamford	Alterations Envil House, Staffordshire
	Mr Bridgens	Repairs to Wine Vaults, London
1774	Mr Corbet	Sundorn House, Salop
	Mr Morhall	Onslow House, Salop
	Mr Taylor	Walton House, Staffordshire
	Earl Manvers	House at Parlthorp, Nottinghamshire
	Mr Corbet	Castle at Sundorn
	Lady St Aubyn	The Wick, Richmond, Surrey
1775	Mr Benyon	Guidea Hall, Romford
	Lady St Aubyn	Work at Clowance House
	Mr Smith	Farmhouse, Oxon
	Admiralty	Work at Greenwich Hospital
	Bishop of Durham	Repairs Durham Cathedral
1776	Mr Trecothick	Monument
	Bishop of Durham	Alterations Aukland castle
1777	Mr Crewe	Alterations to House at Chester
	Mr N. Hill	Designs for House - Cleveland Court
	Sir Abraham Hume	Alterations at Hill Street
	Mr Crewe	New Room, Bolesworth Castle
1778	Dean and Chapter	Repairs to Rochester Cathedral
1779	Mr Trecothick	A poor House
	Mr Hooker	House at Brenchley
1780	Sir Robert Cotton	House at Comber Meers
	Mr Lloyd	Aston House, Salop
	Mr Powys	Alterations near Shrewsbury
	Mr Pigot	Alterations to Rectory. Edgemond
	Dean and Chapter	Roof to Rochester Cathedral
	Mr Durand	House at Carshalton
1783	Mr Mytton	Spire to Halston Park Church, Salop
	Dr Hunter	Museum at Glasgow
1784	Deacon Mellis	Market - Edinburgh
	Vestry Committee	Repairs to Bow Church

	Dr Orme	Alterations to Lambeth Abbey
1785	Dr Law	Repairs Chatham Church
1786	Lady Mary Duncan	Burial Vault
	Mr Smith	Alterations to Putney Hill House
	Vestry Committee	Repairs to Islington Church
1787	Mr Durand	Greyhound Inn, Carshalton
	Mr Smith	Gateway - Somerset
	Mr Murray	Alterations to House in Fleet Street
1788	Mr Kinlock	Two Counting Houses
	Lady A. Clavering	Alterations
1789	Duke of Argyll	Custom House, Tobermory
	Lord Breadalbane	Stables - Taymouth
	Lord Breadalbane	Alterations, 2 cottages - Taymouth
1790	Mr Mackenzie	Inn at Tobermory
	Duke of Argyll	Repairs - House at Ealing
1791	Mr Berners	Obelisk, Wolverstone, Suffolk
	Mr Dance	Survey of Somerset House
	Mr Sayer	House at Richmond
	Mr Campbell	Alterations - Wilmington - Kent
	Lady Derby	Repairs House at Isleworth
	Mr Trecothick	Stables and additions - Addington
1792	Mrs Hammond	Brewhouse in Borough
	Parish Wardens	Repairs to Dartford Church
1794	Mr Dance	Survey of Dome at the Bank
	Mr Mylne	Houses at Amwell
	Mr Webb	Steeple of St Nicholas, Gloucester
1795	Mrs Coxhead	Farm at Ronsham
1797	Mr Cowper	Altering House at Tewin
1798	Mr Patteson	Brewery - Yarmouth
	Mr Edwards	Work at Exton. Rutland
	Mr Burley	Work at Exton. Rutland
	Mr Campbell	Survey Highcliffe - Hants
1798	Mr Evans	Repairs House in Poultry
1799	Stationers Co.	New Front and Roof to Hall
1801	Sir George Evelyn	Aditions to House at Buxted
	Mr Coutts	Alterations to 1 Stratton Street
1802	Mr Trotter	Alterations to Dyrham Park
	Lord Bute	Alterations to Luton Hoo
	Duke of Northumberland	Boating House at Sion
1804	Lord Bute	Alterations at Petersham
1805	Nelson's Funeral	Decorations in St Pauls
		Sir Christopher Wren's Monument
1806	Mr Fergusson	Additions to House
1807	Sir Richard Glynne	Plans for Bethlehem
	Trustees	Survey of British Museum
	Sir Francis Burdett	Alterations to House in Piccadilly
	Mr Coutts	Alterations to House in Wimbledon
1808	Archbishop of Canterbury	Additions to Addington
	Mr Gosling	House at Twickenham
1809	Duke of Northumberland	Work at Isleworth
	Mr Elverton	Almshouses at Ledsbury
	Mr Dance	New Market at Smithfield
	Archbishop of Canterbury	Repairs to St Pauls
	Bishop of London	Jubilee Decorations
1810	Farer and Co	Survey of Lansdowne House

Main Source

Many years back, on the advice of the late Sir John Summerson, I chose Robert Mylne to be the subject of my thesis for qualification as an architect. The late Miss J.M.H. Mylne allowed me full access to all family papers including the volumes of Mylne's Journals 1762-1810, which I transcribed in full.

The thesis was completed in 1953 and, during the next four years, eight of my articles on Mylne were published in Country Life, The Architectural Review and Archaeologia Aeoliana.

I had approached Prof. Sir Albert Richardson for access to his collection of Mylne's architectural drawings, only to be refused. In 1955 he published "Robert Mylne. Architect and Engineer." (Batsford) illustrated with photos and some of the drawings in his collection but, more profusely, with his own inimitable casual pen sketches which did less than credit to either author or subject.

Richardson's book, far from being a biography, contained a brief essay on the man and his work and excerpts from Mylne's Journals, all slapdash and inaccurate. Whilst describing Mylne as a genius on the one hand, Richardson compared him unfavourably with Sir William Chambers and James Wyatt on the other, ignoring Robert Adam meanwhile.

In researching Mylne's work at Inverary, I managed to identify - from his journals - many of the unsigned drawings there to be his authorship, later to be confirmed by Lindsay and Cosh (1979) and Ruddock (1979).

When Maisie Mylne died, her nephew approached me for advice as to where the Journals should be lodged. I recommended the Royal Institute of British Architects, of which I was a member, and gather they have been there for five years, as yet uncatalogued.

The whereabouts of the Richardson collection of Mylne drawings are now unknown, regrettably. Seemingly, Mylne still suffers from a conspiracy to deny him full recognition. Yet others - Prof. Derek Poole of the Welsh School of Architecture, Cardiff University for instance - are intent upon restoration of his well-deserved reputation as indeed so am I.

More will be heard of Robert Mylne before long.

Selected Bibliography

1.   Arch Bridges and Their Builders 1735-1835. Ted Ruddock. 1979. C.U.P.
2.   Inverary and The Dukes of Argyll. Lindsay and Cosh. 1973. E.U.P.
3.   Thomas Telford and The Gloucester and Berkeley Canal.
      G. Neville Crawford. 1989. Industrial Archaeology Review XL2
4.   The History of Gloucester Docks. M. Stimpson. 1980.
5.   The Gloucester and Sharpness Canal. C.P. and C.R. Weaver. 1967.
6.   Gloucester Docks. H. Conway-Jones. 1988.
      Alan Sutton and Gloucester Library Series.
7.   British Canals. Charles Hadfield. 1950. Phoenix House.
8.   The Inland Waterways of England. L.C.T. Rolt. 1950. Allen and Unwin.
9.   The Canal Builders. Anthony Burton. 1972. Eyre Methuen.
10.   The Smeatonians. Garth Watson. 1989. Telford Press.
11.   Thomas Telford. B. Bracegirdle and P.M. Miles. 1973.
      David and Charles.
12.   William Jessop. Charles Hadfield and A.W. Skempton. 1979.
      David and Charles.
13.   The Thames and Severn Canal. Humphrey Household. 1969.
      David and Charles.
14.   The Lost Canals of England. R. Russell. 1971. David and Charles
15.   The Grand Junction Canal. A.H. Faulkner. 1972. David and Charles.
16.   English Canals Part II. Gladwin and White. Undated. Self-published.

Acknowledgements

To British Waterways, in past and present guise, and its staff I owe thanks, in particular to Tony Conder, Curator of the National Waterways Museum, for help and encouragement, to Vanessa Wiggins, Marketing Executive, and the Photo Library, Watford, and especially to Roy Jameson, Archivist at Llantony Warehouse. Likewise the Ironbridge Gorge Museum, the House of Lords Library, The Institution of Civil Engineers, and The Smeatonian Society.

Dr A.S. Brendall of Emmanuel College, Cambridge has been unstinting in help with copies of entries from her Dictionary of Land Surveyors. Thanks also to Gloucester City Library and County Records Office, Cambridge University Press, The National Portrait Gallery, The Commission for Ancient Monuments for Scotland, The Duke of Argyll, Ted Ruddock and Stanley Holland.

A special debt of gratitude to David Lee whose comments on the draft proved invaluable. Nor must I forget the many canal historians, Charles Hadfield in particular, without whose research and publications my contra-thesis would have been impossible.

Finally, without the help of David and Ian Springham this book could not have been published.

Acknowledgement of Illustrations

British Waterways.
    Cover, 4a & b, 5a (with E. Lloyd), 8a & b, 10a (with D. Pratt), 17, 18, 21a & b, 22a & b, 23a (with Gloucester Newspapers Ltd), 23b, 24a & b, 25b, 26b, 29a, b & e, 30b (with Leslie Bryce).
The Duke of Argyll.
    9a, 11, 12, 25a.
Gloucester City Library.
    Frontispiece, 10b.
Ironbridge Gorge Museum Trust.
    19, 20.
Ted Ruddock.
    26a.
Stanley Holland.
    29c & d.
Derek Pratt.
    30a.
Remaining plates.
    Author's collection.

INDEX